MW00467117

The
Billion Dollar BET

The
Billion Dollar BET

ROBERT JOHNSON AND THE INSIDE STORY OF BLACK ENTERTAINMENT TELEVISION

BRETT PULLEY

WILEY

JOHN WILEY & SONS, INC.

Published by John Wiley & Sons, Inc., Hoboken, New Jersey.
Published simultaneously in Canada.

For general information on our other products and services, or technical support, please contact our Customer Care Department within the United States at 800-762-2974, outside the United States at 317-572-3993 or fax 317-572-4002.

Wiley also publishes its books in a variety of electronic formats. Some content that appears in print may not be available in electronic books.

For more information about Wiley products, visit our web site at www.wiley.com.

Library of Congress Cataloging-in-Publication Data:
Pulley, Brett.
    The billion dollar BET : Robert Johnson and the inside story of
Black Entertainment Television / Brett Pulley.
        p.   cm.
"Published simultaneously in Canada."
    ISBN 0-471-42363-7 (cloth)
    1. Black Entertainment Television—History.   2. Television
broadcasting—United States.   3. Johnson, Robert, 1946 April 8–   4.
Executives—United States—Biography.   I. Title.
HE8700.8 .P85 2004
384.55'5'092—dc22

                                        2003026688

Printed in the United States of America.

10 9 8 7 6 5 4 3 2 1

For my wife, Stacey
And our daughters, Zoë and Blake
With love

CONTENTS

"BOOTYLICIOUS"

I t is June 19, 2001, and Las Vegas Boulevard, better known as "the Strip," is packed with people. As the sun sets on another steaming hot day, the hordes of tourists, gawkers, and gamblers begin their night crawl—searching for jackpots and marveling at the man-made spectacles found at the entrances to the many casinos. There's an erupting volcano, a replica of the Brooklyn Bridge, and even a pirate ship that sinks underwater with its real-life crew standing on the deck. But on this evening, there's another spectacle in Las Vegas. Tonight, this gambling town serves as the perfect venue for a flashy, star-studded party thrown by a man who has just received a grand payoff from a very modest bet.

Street teams, the guerrilla marketers usually found in big cities, are out in force, stapling colorful posters on utility poles and walls, announcing the impending release of upcoming albums by the soul artists Usher and Babyface. Outside the Paris Las Vegas Hilton, where a replica of the Eiffel Tower rises 50 stories into the arid Nevada sky, hundreds of well-coiffed and meticulously dressed black people are arriving in limos and taxicabs, filling the entrance to the vast casino floor.

The crowd grows even larger as it moves through the lobby toward the casino's Le Theatre des Arts. "Any extra tickets?" a woman calls out to no one in particular. A young man in a baggy baby blue velour sweat suit, holding a stack of self-recorded compact discs and accompanied by three other similarly dressed men, pleads, "We just want to get in to get somebody to listen to our CD." He and his friends, he promises, are the next big act in hip-hop.

This night, however, is reserved for those who are already stars.

Inside the theater, television production crews are setting up for the First Annual BET Awards, a live two-hour cable telecast honoring African-American performers in music, film, and sports. Among those already inside are the singer and actress Whitney Houston and basketball star Shaquille O'Neal. Ballad king Luther Vandross, known for his smooth falsetto and his huge weight swings, walks in looking as svelte as ever. He takes a front row seat. Kenneth "Babyface" Edmonds and his wife, Tracy, dash down the aisle to their seats. Out in the lobby, the rapper Snoop Dogg arrives with his crew, all of them wearing baseball caps with stocking caps sticking out from underneath. Snoop, wearing rhinestone-studded sunglasses, smiles broadly and weaves through the crowd, posing for photos with anyone who asks, and graciously shaking every hand he can reach.

For the cable channel known as Black Entertainment Television (BET), it's a momentous, watershed occasion. The awards show, which cost $2 million to produce, is the most lavish and expensive entertainment program ever created in the 21-year history of the network. It will be watched in 2.8 million households, the network's second-largest audience ever, surpassed only by a 1996 exclusive interview with football legend O.J. Simpson following his acquittal in the murder trial of his ex-wife.

But far more than ratings, the event is a coronation for BET. Launched in 1980 with a $15,000 bank loan, BET has toiled for more than two decades as a scrappy, entrepreneurial, African-American owned and operated company. But now, BET has just been sold to the media and entertainment giant Viacom Incorporated for an astounding $3 billion. Tonight's awards show officially marks BET's entrance into the big leagues of mainstream television entertainment.

Although the show has an all-star lineup of performers and presenters, the evening belongs to Robert L. Johnson, the founder, builder, and chief executive of BET. Born to a poor family in rural, segregated Mississippi, Johnson has just a few months earlier orchestrated one of the biggest deals ever in the cable business. At the age of 55, he is now on the Forbes 400 list of the richest people in America, and he is the world's first African-American billionaire.

Johnson walks into the theater, taking a front row seat alongside two of his close friends, the professional boxing promoter Butch Lewis, known for his unconventional fashion sense and street smarts, and Leon Robinson, a black character actor who goes simply by one name, Leon. From up on the stage, one of the show's hosts, comedian Cedric "The Entertainer" Kyles, spots Johnson entering the theater. "Bob Johnson!" Cedric announces into the microphone, dramatically emphasizing each syllable. Then he sums Johnson up with one word: "Tycoon." Johnson, an unimposing, slightly built man who has always been able to slip into a room without being noticed, is now a star himself—the center of attention. He flashes his easy, disarming smile. He has a confident, yet demure countenance, as if he is enjoying the fawning attention, but is at the same time a little embarrassed by it all.

As the show begins, one of the hottest and sexiest girl groups in the country, Destiny's Child, struts on stage singing their top-selling single, "Bootylicious." It is a sleek, rousing production, complete with smoke and pyramids and Las Vegas–style magical illusions. It's later followed by an extravagant display of pyrotechnics and an acrobatic performance by the risqué male singer known as Sisqo. With the smoke still clearing, the other host for the evening, comedian Steve Harvey, walks onstage with a dumbstruck look of amazement on his face. "BET has really come up," he says, referring to the first-rate quality of the show. "Back in the day, ain't no way in the world you would have had all of that money invested in a BET production." Funnyman Cedric chimes in: "Yea, to get that amount of smoke you would have had to hook a raggedy '74 Cordoba up, and keep telling somebody, 'Put it in neutral, hit the gas, we need some more smoke.' "

Since its inception 21 years earlier, BET had a earned a reputation as a low-budget operation that never seemed to show the same quality programming that could be found on most mainstream television outlets. Despite these perceived shortcomings, the network flourished as it became a source of pride for its audience—treasured as the only television outlet owned and operated by black people, and more importantly, devoted to black-oriented programming.

BET's eventual reach into 75 million homes across the United States and its emphasis on music, style, and celebrities turned Johnson into one of the country's most important cultural influences. Because of his network, a fledgling and original musical style known as rap emerged from the ghetto to infiltrate mainstream America and become a major multibillion-dollar business. Because any teenager or young adult with cable could switch on BET, the entire hip-hop culture moved beyond its black urban roots and deeply penetrated white households in suburban and even rural America. A new generation of young, swaggering multimillionaire athletes and entertainers emerged, and BET became the place where the entire country could go to witness this profound cultural shift.

As the network grew, Johnson personally became a beacon for entrepreneurs of all races and a powerful player in the media business. He created a new blueprint for black capitalism. Unlike so many black entrepreneurs before him, he did not worry about his company being perceived as one that consciously uplifted the race. BET did indeed do its share of good deeds, serving its target market well with religious programming and extensive coverage of events like the 1995 Million Man March and the funeral of Ron Brown, the Clinton administration commerce secretary, who was killed in a 1996 plane crash. Yet Johnson never shied from making it clear to anyone who questioned BET's purpose: It was all about making money. And the network made plenty.

The programming that generated the largest profit margins and comprised most of the schedule was music and stand-up comedy. But some of BET's original fans slowly grew to despise the network for its heavy rotation of music videos rife with flashy cars and scantly clad gyrating derrieres, as well as its lowbrow comedy shows. As it became successful, BET garnered both love and contempt in the black community, and Johnson was reviled as much as revered.

In Hollywood, where black writers, actors, and producers had for years felt left out of the mainstream business, BET was criticized for failing to create a major platform for these people. And some performers who did get opportunities at BET still publicly lambasted the network for paying low wages.

Johnson's critics came in all colors. White cable system operators who carried BET complained about the low-budget programming. And business associates whispered among themselves, accusing Johnson of racial opportunism baiting—claiming that he used race to gain advantages in the marketplace while at the same time he demanded that he should have no more responsibility to air programming for social causes than should any mainstream cable channel. His only responsibility, Johnson argued, was to run a profitable business by giving viewers what most of them wanted, and doing it as cheaply as possible. If the black race happened to gain some social benefit from that, then fine.

Johnson often defended himself by claiming that only small, elite classes of people had problems with BET. He insisted that the masses, the 35 million African-American consumers in the

United States, the ones who paid for cable each month and bought the cars and clothes and music advertised on the network, had no complaints.

In a 2001 interview for *Forbes* magazine, Johnson talked about the challenge of running the country's only black-oriented television channel, the criticism that came his way, and how he kept himself and his employees focused on profits:

> We were the only black network. So we became the burden carrier for the black community, with all of its desires about what we should do. We became the burden carrier for the cable operators for all that they wanted us to do. They weren't going to create another black channel to do it, so we had to do it. And then we became the burden carrier for every black person in Hollywood who wanted to have a place to show their wares because the other channels weren't giving them a place. And we became the place for every intellectual who felt that we should be doing more socially relevant matter. Everybody poured their burdens and obligations on BET. So, what we basically said is, "We can't solve everybody's desires for BET. We have to run the business according to what we believe." And for me that was rooted in having to be focused on running this as a business, a profit maximization business.
>
> If you think about this company from day one to today, it created $3 billion in value. That's $150 million of value each year that it existed. That's the result of us doing a few things: having disciplined management that focused on profit maximization, leveraging the equity markets at the right time, and strategic decision making about how to structure the company—when to go public, go private, sell to another company. Those things have been a consistent hallmark of what we've done. The results show that. We took the good fortune of being the first in an industry that was starting up, positioned ourselves in that industry, and took advantage of it.
>
> We were not running a popularity contest for Hollywood. We were not trying to be socially redeeming for black intellectuals.

And we were not trying to solve all the cable operators' problems and ideas about what black programming should be. We were running a business. And we had the right to run our business the same way MTV runs its business, or HBO runs its business or Comedy Central runs its business. So that's the way we did it.[1]

He may have his critics, but as one of the great business trailblazers of all time, Johnson also has legions of fans and admirers. He is credited with creating opportunities for hundreds of young black professionals and turning several of them into millionaires. His purchase of the National Basketball Association's new Charlotte, North Carolina, franchise made him the first African-American owner in professional sports—a major breakthrough as important to the sports front office as was Jackie Robinson's arrival on the playing field. As the basketball legend and entrepreneur Magic Johnson told him: "Bob, I always aspired to be like you. You made it happen for black folks."[2]

This is the first-ever in-depth look at one of the most enigmatic and important entrepreneurs of our time. It is a revealing portrait of a brilliant and relentlessly focused businessman, whose life is a window into race, culture, and capitalism. Much more than the tale of one company, the story of how Johnson built BET is a story about the entire modern media business. As one of the early basic cable channels that came to life when the world was still dominated by broadcast, BET and others like it splintered viewing audiences and grew to become some of the most valuable and desirable properties in the media business.

From his Mississippi roots to his early years in rural Illinois, at Princeton University, and as a lobbyist in Washington, D.C., Johnson has traveled an unimaginable journey. Along the way, he has struck up friendships and formed vital relationships with key people, from Hollywood superstar Denzel Washington and former president Bill Clinton to media titans John Malone and Sumner Redstone.

For the first time ever, here is the unvarnished, inside account of Johnson's life: a man who is disarming with his warm manner and charm, but beneath the surface is singularly focused, icy, and relentless in his pursuit of profits. Like a modern-day *Citizen Kane*, Johnson gains the world, but in the process sacrifices the adoration of others.

Here are the details of the real-life issues, situations, joys, and sorrows that occurred on his road to financial success. Far more than a corporate analysis of profits and losses, it is a story about savvy, vision, timing, determination, fighting, failures, scandals, love, and sex—all the things that occur behind the scenes as a company and its leader grow up. It reveals an ambition and fiery determination that burned so hot that friendships were shattered, family relationships destroyed, and hearts broken.

This is a classic American business tale, of a poor country boy who mixed old-fashioned grit, sweat, and tears to attain unfathomable wealth. This is the story of the greatest $15,000 bet ever made. It is the story of Robert Louis Johnson, and the billion-dollar empire that he built.

THE OTHER SIDE
OF THE TRACKS

It was the dirtiest place on earth.

That's what people used to say, anyway. Of course it was a bit of an exaggeration, or colloquial hyperbole. Nevertheless, in the early 1960s the Burgess Battery plant—11 buildings stretched across six acres hugging the west bank of the murky Pecatonica River—was certainly one of the dirtiest places in all of Freeport, Illinois.

Down in the basement of the main building was where most of the black men employed at the company were relegated. This was also where the filthiest part of the process of manufacturing dry cell batteries took place. A carbon-based substance known as slip mix was dumped into huge vats, hardened, and turned into thin sticks of carbon. This was the central part of a battery, and the sticks, or "pitch," as they were called, were made in different sizes, depending on the type of battery they were to be used for. Burgess made virtually all kinds of batteries, from common household cells for companies like Ray-O-Vac and EverReady to huge emergency powerpacks for hospitals and high-voltage batteries for mobile radio receivers used by the military.

The pitch sticks were loaded onto rolling hoppers and transported up to the fourth floor, where the dirty work continued.

There the workers, many of them women, stood along conveyor belts, dropping the carbon sticks into aluminum tubes, then sealing the casings closed.

Throughout the process, the black, gritty carbon stuck to everything. If the carbon got on a worker's hands, that worker could forget about scratching an itch or touching his or her face without getting smudged and marked up like a coal miner. Workers wore special boots and rubber gloves, and they scrubbed at huge washbasins after each shift. Still, the grime prevailed. "The dirt was so pervasive," recalls Geraldine Jones, who worked at the plant, "people really didn't want anyone from Burgess getting into their car. It was a filthy thing."

In 1965, at the age of 19, Robert L. Johnson landed a summer job at Burgess, where he soon discovered he was not cut out for taking orders and working for someone else. The company had a hiring policy that gave preference to the children of its workers, and because Johnson's mother, Edna, worked at the plant, he, too, got a job. Each day, Johnson climbed the main building's metal stairs to the second floor, where all workers punched the primary clock. Then he proceeded to the fourth floor, where he was required to punch yet another clock, the department clock, officially starting his pay period.

The minimum wage job was simple enough. As the workers dropped the pitch into the aluminum tubes, carbon dust would fall under the conveyor belt onto the floor and Johnson had to sweep it up. From the start, he hated the grimy, mindless work, and developed a system for himself that made it easier to bear. He'd let the dirt accumulate, sweep it up, then kill time socializing with other workers. The foreman, of course, did not like Johnson's system.

"Keep the floor constantly swept," the foreman ordered.

Johnson refused. What difference did it make, he argued, as long as the floor was clean at the end of the day?

Fed up with his obstinate young employee, the foreman approached Johnson one Wednesday during a shift. "You know, Johnson," he said, "Friday is your last day."

"No, Friday is not my last day," Johnson replied.

"What do you mean?" the foreman asked.

"*Today* is my last day," Johnson declared.

As Johnson gathered his belongings before leaving the plant, the foreman made a suggestion. "If you're going to get a job, you'd better work for yourself," the foreman said. "Working for other people just doesn't seem to be your cup of tea because you've got a unique way of how you want to do things."[1] The foreman's words stayed with Johnson for years to come. More than mere advice, they were sheer prophecy.

When Robert Louis Johnson was born on April 8, 1946, in Hickory, Mississippi, the future held little promise for a black boy greeted with open arms by poverty, poor education, and oppression. He would be known to his family as Bobby, but his formal first name came from a great-uncle, Robert C. Johnson. The origin of his great-uncle's middle initial underscores the times in which the early generations of Johnsons lived. There were two other Robert Johnsons, both white, who resided in the Hickory area around the turn of the century, so in order to keep the black Robert distinguished from the white Roberts, Johnson's great-uncle adopted "Colored" as his middle name.

Located 60 miles east of Jackson, Hickory in those days was home to about 650 people, and the Johnson family alone accounted for a large number of the residents. Bobby was the ninth of 10 children born to Edna and Archie Johnson. Both of his parents grew up five miles outside of Hickory, deep in the sticks, in a small community called Good Hope. Johnson's great-grandfather, Filmore Johnson, who had been born into slavery, planted the first seeds of self-sufficiency in the family. A man ahead of his time, Filmore managed to purchase dozens of acres of land for his family in Good Hope. Farming was the primary source of income in the area, and there were a couple of cotton gins and some small dairies. With the abundance of forestland, there was also a sawmill that produced lumber and a stave mill that made barrels for storing whiskey.

Filmore Johnson farmed on his land and he traded at the local general store. Robert "Johnnie" Brand, whose white family ran the store, recalls Filmore in the 1930s arriving at the store on a horse-pulled buggy and loading up staples like huge sacks of sugar and barrels of flour to take home. Sometimes Brand would ride a bicycle to deliver goods to Filmore and his wife, Betty. He'd follow a dirt trail about a mile off the road, and when he reached the house, Betty would greet him with freshly made cakes and pies. "I was a little boy, and I called her 'Aunt Betty,'" says Brand, who is now in his late seventies. "To call her Aunt meant that she was someone who we had respect for. The Johnsons were poor, working people. But they were nice, good people."

Filmore was known as a proud, stubborn man. Once he fixed his mind on doing something a certain way, nothing and no one could dissuade him. It was a personality trait that would pass down through the generations. When a descendant was caught being particularly bullheaded, someone might note, "That's the Filmore showing up." Once, after they were well along in age, Betty became so tired of Filmore's hardheaded ways that she moved out of the house and into a nearby place of her own. But shortly thereafter they made up and were back together. Filmore died at age 86 in 1945, and Betty died seven years later, in her early nineties.

Their grandson, Archie, did not go very far in school, but he followed Filmore's legacy of self-sufficiency. Archie, who was Bobby's father, provided for his large family mostly by cutting and selling wood. Known to everyone by his nickname "Peck," Archie Johnson drove a pickup truck, hauling pulpwood to nearby railroad yards, where it was loaded onto trains and taken to pulp mills to be turned into lumber, paper, and other downstream products. The truck provided a means of self-employment for Archie: Anytime he needed a little cash, he'd go and cut some wood, take it to the rail yard, and sell it.

As a small boy in the South during the early 1950s, Bobby lived in a segregated world in and around Hickory. The town's population was evenly split along racial lines, and everything from water fountains to classrooms were separated based on race. His mother, Edna, taught children at an all-black, one-room school in Good Hope. Yet even after Good Hope's schools consolidated with the school district in Hickory in the 1950s, the students remained segregated and Edna continued to teach elementary grades at an all-black school in Hickory.

Race relations were "pretty rough," recalls Johnson's cousin, Tom E. Johnson, who has lived most of his more than 80 years in the Hickory area. "Everybody got along because you knew what you had to do." In the early 1960s, when three civil rights workers were killed just 35 miles away from Hickory in the small town of Philadelphia, the FBI agents who descended on the state to investigate the famous case questioned residents in Hickory. The murders became a flashpoint in the nation's struggle with race, underscoring Mississippi's entrenched resistance to the civil rights movement and defining the state for years as a bastion of racism.

By the time that Dr. Martin Luther King Jr. was delivering his historic 1963 "I Have a Dream" speech, in which he referred to Mississippi as "a state sweltering with the heat of injustice," Archie and Edna Johnson had already packed up their 10 children and their belongings and headed north.

Like so many Southern blacks who pursued better lives in the industrial areas of the Midwest, they followed the path of the Illinois Central Railroad, finally settling 150 miles northwest of Chicago in Freeport, Illinois, a rural town of factories and farms.

Freeport, host to one of the famous debates between Abraham Lincoln and Stephen Douglas in their 1858 Senate race, had a population of 26,000 residents, less than 10 percent of whom were black. Many of the black residents worked at factories like Newell Manufacturing, the maker of Rubbermaid Products. Some of these factories, such as the Kraft cheese plant, were not yet hiring many black workers when the Johnsons arrived. Beyond the factories, many blacks worked on the railroad, cleaning trains, shoveling coal, and serving as dining car porters.

The Pecatonica River and the Illinois Central Railroad tracks were next to each other, running parallel through town and separating the west side from the east side and, for the most part, whites from blacks. Most of the town's black residents lived on the east side. Some black homes spilled over onto the west side, but just barely. Most of the blacks who were on the white side of town were within 100 yards of the railroad tracks. They lived close to the tracks, many people surmised, because they arrived from the South on the trains and thus settled near where they got off.

Blacks shared their dilapidated neighborhoods with a sizable group of Italian immigrants who had come in search of Freeport's industrial opportunities. The Johnsons over a period of many years lived in a succession of old rental homes on the east side, mostly in and around an area that people disdainfully called the "3-D" neighborhood. It stood for dagos, darkies, and dogs.

Archie found work at W. T. Rawleigh, a liniment, cosmetics, and spice manufacturer that occupied a vast six-story redbrick complex along the river. Each day, the factory's smokestacks emitted a different aroma, which would waft with the wind and fill the quaint downtown air with the smell of butterscotch, vanilla, and countless other flavorings and seasonings. Just as the Johnsons were known as enterprising people back in Hickory, Archie gained the same reputation in Freeport. Between factory jobs, he drove his small truck, salvaging junk in and around town. Edna, meanwhile, worked at Burgess Battery, and later for the Micro Switch division of Honeywell.

The couple managed to keep their large family clothed and fed. Archie's wife, whom people called "Miss Edna," watched over their clan and earned money as a hairstylist working inside her home. Archie would sometimes return to Hickory to visit with friends and family, and to cut and haul more wood. A short, slightly built man, Archie—like his grandfather Filmore—could be stubborn and headstrong. But he also had a fun-loving nature. In later years, one of Bobby's buddies accompanied him home for a visit and slept in the bed that belonged to Johnson's older sister, Paulette. In the middle of the night, Archie decided to play a practical joke on the unsuspecting houseguest. Standing outside the bedroom door, Archie started shouting and feigning anger. "Who's that man in Paulette's bed?" he yelled. He frightened Bobby's poor friend nearly to death.

Archie also found time to, as one old friend who asked to remain anonymous delicately put it, "kind of meander around." Once, a neighbor in Freeport offered to give the Johnsons a huge deep freezer—free of charge. With all the mouths that Archie and Edna were feeding, an extra place to store food sounded quite useful. All they had to do was go to the neighbor's home and haul the freezer away. Archie dutifully arrived at the neighbor's place and loaded the freezer onto his truck. But instead of taking it home to Edna and the children, Archie took the freezer and presented it, as a gift, to another lady friend. Despite such episodes over the years, the Johnson family remained close-knit. It was not until many years later, once all of their children were grown, that Archie and Edna divorced after 36 years of marriage. He later remarried, and Edna remained single for the remainder of her life.

Bobby began working hard at an early age. The summer position at Burgess Battery was not his first job, nor was it his first exposure to dirty work. As a young teen, he was hired by one of his neighbors to work at the nearby Stephenson County Fairgrounds each summer. While local residents were enjoying the livestock competitions, the carnival, and the country music, Bobby was working as a roustabout, removing cow and horse manure from the animal pens and keeping the public bathrooms clean. He also earned money mowing lawns around Freeport. "I always worked," Johnson said in a 2002 article in *Fortune Small Business*. "I was not afraid of getting my hands dirty."[2] He even tried operating a newspaper route, delivering the *Rockford Morning Star*. Trying to collect payments from recalcitrant subscribers and walking up and down the streets on Freeport's bone-chilling mornings proved to be more than he could stand, however. Eventually, one of his older brothers took over the route. It was the only time that Johnson would fail as a businessman.

For Bobby and other black kids growing up in Freeport in those days, the best that the future had to offer was limited in scope. A job at one of the factories; a modest house on the black side of town; and Friday nights reserved for partying, drinking, cursing, and fighting seemed to be about as good as it would ever get. "Get an education" is what Bobby and other young black kids like himself kept hearing from their elders. But the legacy of poor education within the families created a vicious circle: The children often found themselves following the paths of their parents—unsure about how to get into college, unable to pay for it, and consequently locked in, at a young age, to a lifetime of menial work.

The only way out, it seemed, was through the military or sports. And Bobby and his three brothers were athletic and competitive. One of Bobby's best friends at the time, Preston Pearson, recalls that he and his own brothers competed fiercely against the Johnson boys throughout grade school. Pearson, who at Freeport High School was a standout in football, basketball, and track and field, went on to play for the

Dallas Cowboys and the Pittsburgh Steelers. Over a 15-year career in the National Football League, Pearson played in five Super Bowl games.

At Freeport High School, Bobby also ran track and played on the football team and the basketball team. "I wouldn't say he was Michael Jordan," Pearson says jokingly. "But he played." Standing at little more than five and a half feet and weighing about 150 pounds with his winter coat on, Bobby realized early on that he'd have to find another ticket out of Freeport. "Even back then," Pearson recalls, "his long-term thoughts had that intellectual bent. He was a very deep thinker."[3] Even the older people around Freeport noticed that Johnson was awfully serious-minded and uncommonly self-assured for his age. Almeada Jones, an elderly woman who lived a couple of homes down the road from the Johnsons, would observe her young neighbor and predict: "He's gonna amount to something."

Where Bobby excelled most was in the classroom. Whites and blacks in Freeport attended the same high school, but over 90 percent of the students at the school were white. It was an environment that taught Johnson early on how to socialize, compete, and succeed in a setting where he was often the only black person, as was the case in many of his classes and in after-school activities. He was friendly and engaging, and seemed confident and comfortable around everyone. "He was one who would not make a lot of noise to be recognized," recalls Lyle Reedy, who was the dean of boys at the school. "He went about his way. I don't remember ever having to discipline him."

By the time he reached his senior year in 1964, Johnson's grades were so good that he was on his way to graduating with honors. But because none of his brothers or sisters had attended college, he had no plans to do so, either. "The problem was I couldn't afford college, so I hadn't even considered it," Johnson later said. "My destiny was set, I thought. I was going to follow my older brother into the air force. I wanted to become a fighter pilot."[4]

But one day, while sitting in an advanced English class, Johnson's fate was altered when the teacher asked, "How many of you are going to college?" Every hand went up, except for Johnson's. And he was the only black student in the class. As he quickly looked around the room and saw the white kids proudly holding their hands high, he felt "completely embarrassed," he later recalled.[5] "I did not want to be singled out, so I raised my hand." The teacher was persistent in the coming weeks, requiring each of the students to see a guidance counselor and follow through with the application process. Because Johnson had raised his hand to avoid embarrassment, he was now forced to pursue college. The problem was he had no idea where to apply.

His buddy Pearson, however, had graduated from Freeport the previous year and gone off to the University of Illinois on a basketball scholarship. So Johnson called Pearson and the two arranged for Johnson to visit the campus in Champaign, Illinois. After the visit, Johnson applied and was accepted. The tuition was just $224 a semester for state residents, but to pay for room and board he took out a low-interest student loan and got a job cleaning a microbiology lab on campus.

It was a fortuitous twist of fate. Because he was smart enough to be sitting there in that advanced English class when the teacher asked a simple question, Robert L. Johnson, the ninth of 10 children, was now the first one who was college bound. The cycle of poor education within his family was broken, and Johnson had learned a vital lesson. From that day on, throughout his life, he would seize opportunities that came his way simply because he was in the right room, with the right people, at the right time. "It is being in what I call the deal flow," Johnson later said, relating the phenomenon to the business world. "You are there inside the room when deals are get-

ting done. All of this happens within the white world on a regular basis. But there are few black people who are regularly in
that deal flow."[6]

When he arrived on the University of Illinois campus in
1964, the civil rights movement was in full swing, and there was
plenty of racial tension on the campus. The small fraction of the
college's students who were black always watched their backs, as
it was not beneath their white classmates to get drunk and become verbally abusive.

Many of the black students on campus were from Chicago
and its suburbs. Some had been raised in the street-smart ways
of the city's predominantly black urban neighborhoods. Others hailed from the city's large and sophisticated black bour-
geoisie families headed by doctors, lawyers, teachers, and
small-business owners. Johnson, on the other hand, was one of
the few hayseeds, seemingly naive and countrified compared
to many of his classmates. Yet his innocence and friendly manner were assets.

"He wasn't slick at all," recalls Virgil Hemphill, who roomed
with Johnson their freshman year. "But he had a nice personality
and could talk to anybody. He would keep you laughing." Johnson would joke about how large his family was, or sometimes he
made Freeport the butt of his jokes. He and Pearson would laugh
about how they could not wait to catch the "first thing smoking"
to get away from their hometown. Johnson would warn other
students: "If you're ever on a train and it goes through Freeport,
don't get off."

Johnson majored in history, and during his first year on campus he followed in Pearson's footsteps and joined a popular black
fraternity, Kappa Alpha Psi. Members of the fraternity, which
was founded in 1911 on the campus of Indiana University,
taught all young initiates that high achievement should be their
primary goal in college and throughout life. One of the nation's
largest black fraternities, Kappa Alpha Psi has inducted over

120,000 men into its ranks, including famous members such as tennis legend Arthur Ashe, the famous defense attorney Johnnie Cochran, and basketball legends Bill Russell and Wilt Chamberlin.[7]

While at Illinois, Johnson lived at the Kappa house, along with Pearson, Hemphill, and other members. Through the fraternity, he gained one of his first lessons in leadership, serving as the chapter's president. He also served one year as the frat's social chairman. This was a job of the highest order. For although the fraternity brothers took great pride in their charitable work in the local community, there was little doubt about who *really* had the most important responsibility in the frat. Everyone knew it was the social chairman—the guy in charge of throwing the parties. The Kappas fancied themselves as suave, fun-loving playboys, and Johnson and his brothers had plenty of parties and good times inside the small, clapboard dwelling that served as their official frat house.

But for Johnson, the good times got out of hand. Before new members could join the fraternity, they were required to go through a long and rigorous pledge period that could last several weeks and often included physical and mental hazing. On one occasion, a pledging ritual escalated and Johnson was accused by a fellow member of physically hazing an initiate, or "scroller," as the young pledges were dubbed. The national arm of the fraternity had become zealous in its efforts to put an end to hazing incidents, and after the charges against Johnson were investigated, the ultimate punishment was exacted: He was expelled from the fraternity. Little did it matter to many of the organization's brothers, however, because once a man was "made," or taught all of the rituals and secrets shared by members, there was in practical terms no undoing it. Still, it was a harsh and cruel rejection for Johnson.

During Johnson's junior year he met a pretty black freshman named Sheila Crump, who hailed from an upper-middle-class, suburban Chicago family. Crump, the daughter of a neurosurgeon, had been a cheerleader at a predominantly white high school in Maywood, Illinois, and was a violin virtuoso, having studied the instrument since her early childhood. She was on a music scholarship at Illinois and she became the university's first black female cheerleader.

Around the same time, Johnson learned of a new effort to attract minorities into the field of foreign service. Funded by the Ford Foundation, the program would pay for graduate school for anyone who completed a foreign service program with the U.S. State Department. Johnson applied to the Woodrow Wilson School at Princeton University and was accepted. He would ultimately bypass the foreign service, however, as Princeton's master's in public administration program was fully funded by a foundation that provided full scholarships and funding to the entire student body. Designed to train future government leaders, the two-year program attracted a small, yet elite group of students each year. Among those who attended during Johnson's days were the author Taylor Branch and former U.S. ambassador to the United Nations Richard Holbrooke.

The graduate school was making its first real push to attract black students, and for Johnson and the four or five other black students who were among the total class of about 70 students, it was a difficult existence. Located in central New Jersey, the elite Ivy League university was very white and filled with neoliberals who could sometimes be condescending toward the new black students. It was September 1968, the Vietnam War was raging, and Martin Luther King Jr. had been slain months earlier. While the white students in Johnson's class were pinning on peace signs and protesting the war, most of their black counterparts were congregating among themselves, captivated by the nation's black power movement and asserting, for the first time in their lives, that their blackness was a source of pride, a thing of beauty. For the white students, this newfound black power was confusing and disconcerting.

"It was pretty hard for the black students and the white students to make it work," recalls James B. Lindheim, a white classmate of Johnson's. "There was a black and white thing going on. For those of us trying to be liberal, it was like 'How do I relate to this?' There was a big wall, and it wasn't easy to get across it."

Johnson was not notably active in the black power movement. He was his regular cordial and charming self, but some of his classmates thought he was unusually quiet. For the first time in his life, it seemed, he was struggling academically. "We thought he was a cool guy, but we weren't sure that he was that effective as a student or as a member of the student community," recalls classmate Michael Aron. "We all liked him, but we could see he was kind of treading water."

The rigorous Ivy League academics may have been a contributing factor, but Johnson had something far greater on his mind: Sheila Crump. He was in love, and totally distracted by it. Instead of focusing on his studies, he spent a lot of time on the telephone, calling Sheila back at the University of Illinois, running up expensive phone bills.

Unfocused on his studies, Johnson dropped out. In 1969, as he and Sheila exchanged vows on the campus where they had met two years earlier, Johnson formed his first major partnership: Robert and Sheila Johnson. While Sheila stayed at Illinois to complete her studies and receive her bachelor's degree in music, Johnson found work 150 miles away as a high school teacher on Chicago's South Side. Although he had earlier considered teaching as a career, his ambition had now grown much larger. His new life with Sheila introduced him to a whole new class of highly successful and affluent black professionals. His bride's upper-middle-class background gave him great incentive and made him ever more determined to prove himself to both Sheila and her family, and to distance himself from his lowly, blue-collar background.

Content that he now had a ring on Sheila's finger, Johnson refocused on graduate school. He returned to Princeton and in 1972 he received his master's degree in public administration. Johnson was now fully prepared to accomplish far greater things.

ACCESS TO POWER

B
ob and Sheila moved to Washington, D.C., where she briefly worked as a research analyst on Capitol Hill and he found a job that introduced him to the television industry. Serving as the public affairs director for the Corporation for Public Broadcasting, he began to learn firsthand of the power and untapped potential of television. Around the same time he also worked as the director of communications for the Washington, D.C., office of the National Urban League, the civil rights group that focuses on black economic empowerment. The combination—broadcasting and black economic welfare—presaged the course his life would take.

The Urban League's dynamic leader, Whitney Young, had recently drowned while in Nigeria, and the lawyer and head of the United Negro College Fund, Vernon Jordan, had just been named the new chief. During Johnson's brief tenure, the director of the D.C. office, Sterling Tucker, was temporarily assigned to the national office, working with Jordan in a failed bid to convince the Nixon administration to adopt a domestic Marshall Plan aimed at rebuilding urban America following the civil unrest of the 1960s, just as the original Marshall Plan rebuilt Europe following World War II.

Johnson dealt with public affairs and media relations, but those who got to know him sensed his ambition. "He had real dreams back then," recalls Tucker. "He would talk about business-related things that back then black folks weren't doing. I was sometimes bored to death with Bob as he would talk so long about things that seemed like pie in the sky. I would say, 'Yeah, that's great, Bob, but we have some real problems that we have to deal with today.' But he had this thing of becoming a wealthy man on his mind." In 1973, the contacts Johnson had made work-ing for Tucker helped him land a job on Capitol Hill as press sec-retary for U.S. congressman Walter E. Fauntroy, the Washington, D.C., minister and civil rights leader who had been elected to Congress two years earlier.

Fauntroy was in the early phase of his congressional career and would go on to serve 10 terms in the House of Represen-tatives. Still, by the time Johnson arrived in his office, the con-gressman was already a well-recognized leader. He had won a Washington, D.C., citywide high school oratory contest at the age of 17, and went on to graduate from the Yale Univer-sity divinity school. He then returned to the Washington Bap-tist church where he had been raised and became its pastor. In the early 1960s Fauntroy was selected by Dr. Martin Luther King as a key Washington point person for the civil rights struggle, and as a result he helped organize the 1963 march on Washington where King delivered his immortal "I Have a Dream" speech. Soon thereafter, Fauntroy was picked by Pres-ident Lyndon B. Johnson as a vice chairman of an effort that oversaw the implementation of the landmark Civil Rights Act of 1964 and the Voting Rights Act of 1965. In 1971 at the age of 37, Fauntroy, a Democrat, became the first person elected to Congress to represent the city of Washington after nearly a century in which it had lacked its own congressional delegation.

Fauntroy's office provided a heady environment for Johnson, who was now 26 years old. Constantly meeting and mixing with famous and powerful people inside the corridors of Capitol Hill,

Bob Johnson was, as folks back in Mississippi used to say, "in high cotton."

Johnson was energetic and focused as he went about his responsibilities, which involved things like writing and issuing press releases, and arranging media briefings and interviews for the congressman. "Bob did a lot of little things and was very helpful," Fauntroy recalls.[1]

One person with whom Johnson worked closely in the office was Delano E. Lewis, who served as the congressman's chief of staff. Like Johnson, Lewis had come from meager means. He had been raised in Kansas, his father a railroad porter and his mother a maid. After finishing law school at the University of Kansas, Lewis had worked several jobs in Washington, including a stint in the Kennedy administration's Department of Justice and another as a staff member with the black Republican senator from Massachusetts, Edward Brooke. Lewis, who was five or six years older than Johnson, had already gained a fair amount of polish and proved the perfect friend to help Johnson navigate the ways of Washington.

Washington at the time did not have its own elected city officials. There was no city council, and the mayor was appointed by Congress. Because of the city's lack of statehood, Fauntroy was elected as a nonvoting delegate to Congress; but he was still the city's highest-ranking elected official. So as Johnson and Lewis went about learning the ways of Capitol Hill and its confusing world of committees and processes, they were also busy with Fauntroy's efforts to help the city gain its own elected government. "Bob and I worked very closely together, and it was chaos," recalls Lewis.[2]

The two men, as Lewis says, became "good friends." Like Johnson, Lewis would go on to become immensely successful in the business world. He became chief executive officer of the former Chesapeake & Potomac Telephone Company, which later became a part of Verizon. He went on to become head of National Public Radio and to serve on many corporate boards, including the banking giant Chase Manhattan and Eastman Kodak. Lewis would also play a vital role in the building of Johnson's future media empire, as a board member of BET.

Johnson was soaking up the experience on Capitol Hill. He began to clearly understand the value of developing a broad array of relationships and the benefit of having the means to communicate instantly with vast numbers of people. Fauntroy, who at the time was trying to make the newly founded Congressional Black Caucus a strong force in legislative matters, had been feeling frustrated that whenever he and other black representatives accomplished something in Congress few people around the country found out about it. "When we did outstanding things, they were smothered," Fauntroy says. "We got some two-minute blurbs" in the media, "but you couldn't cover much in two minutes."

One day in 1976, Johnson told Fauntroy about the nascent cable television business and how it might offer the potential for black leaders like himself to send their messages out via satellite to their constituents around the country. Fauntroy grew excited as Johnson described the possibilities. "That's perfect," Fauntroy exclaimed. "We can have a black educational television network to allow me to visit with my people without using envelopes and stamps. I can have them tuning in and calling in instead of reading," he said, pondering how it might work. "After all, we are a visual people."

Shortly thereafter, what Johnson later called a totally serendipitous event occurred. Attending a party at his next-door neighbor's house and doing his normally expert job of schmoozing, he met a young lady and they started talking. She was an employee of the National Cable Television Association (NCTA), a trade group that had been founded in 1952 as the National Community Television Association and was charged with representing the fledgling cable business. "You'd make a good lobbyist for the cable industry," she said to Johnson. He told her that he didn't know much about the industry. "Don't worry," she replied. "I didn't know much when I joined."[3]

Johnson then met with the head of the agency and was offered a job as vice president in charge of lobbying on behalf of pay television. When he informed Fauntroy that he was leaving his staff, the congressman gave his blessings believing that Johnson might actually make the cable service that they had discussed a reality. "I sent Bob out," Fauntroy now says, as if proudly claiming some degree of responsibility for the success that was to come. But then he adds in a more forlorn tone, "I had great hope" for a black cable channel. "I hoped it would become black educational television so we could use it to educate our people."

More than anything, though, the NCTA position sounded like a good job. In fact, the position had already proven to be extremely beneficial to another black man before Johnson. Four years earlier, in 1972, the cable association had hired Don Anderson to fill the government relations job. Anderson, who had previously been chief executive of a small firm that produced in-flight music for airlines, had the good fortune of applying for the job at just the right time. The government was expected to soon remove restrictions that prevented cable companies from installing their wires in big cities, and the industry would need black professionals to help navigate markets like Chicago, Detroit, and Gary, Indiana. These cities and many others were places that, largely as a result of whites fleeing to the suburbs, now had high concentrations of black residents, and more importantly, were electing black mayors, city managers, and council members. These were the people who would award the cable franchises.

The night before he was to interview for the job, Anderson showed up at Washington's Madison Hotel, where the NCTA was hosting a reception. He had been told that there were more than 200 applicants, so he figured it was such a long shot that he didn't have much to lose by attending. There were hardly any blacks to be found in the industry at the time, and when Anderson walked into the reception he was painfully conspicuous. William Bresnan, a cable industry pioneer who was also on the NCTA board, walked over to Anderson and politely asked in so many words, "What are you doing here?" When Anderson introduced himself and told Bresnan that he was an applicant for the job, the chairman's demeanor instantly changed as the lightbulb went on in his head. "Terrific!" he exclaimed. Less than 24 hours later, Anderson had met the entire NCTA board as well as the organization's president, and had been hired for the job.

So hot a commodity was Anderson that within six months after starting at the NCTA he was getting job offers from the various companies that he was representing on Capitol Hill. About 18 months after joining, he was attending a board meeting when Gerald Levin, the head of a fledgling pay channel known as Home Box Office (HBO), approached him. "We're interested in you and we want you to come aboard," said Levin, who years later would become chief executive of AOL Time Warner. Time Inc. had just finished buying out its partner in the channel, and HBO appeared headed for growth. Anderson took the job and spent the next 17 years at HBO, eventually becoming one of Time Inc.'s first African-American officers. He would also later play a key role in the building of Johnson's fortune.

Once Johnson arrived at the NCTA in 1976, he started his official transformation from the socially minded young man who had considered teaching and the foreign service into the capitalist who made wealth creation his ultimate goal. His primary job at the agency was to lobby lawmakers to lift restrictions that were imposed on companies that wanted to show movies on pay television. At the time, channels like Home Box Office or the Movie Channel were restricted by federal regulations as to what films they could show. For example, there was a somewhat bizarre rule that stipulated that the movies shown on pay television must be either less than two years old or more than 10 years old. This was done to protect the major broadcast networks, which depended heavily on big movie nights for ratings. Emerging media moguls like Barry Diller, who headed ABC at the time, were making their marks by effectively buying theatrical releases and scheduling them on their networks. By keeping the eight-year window carved out for the networks, the government assured the broadcasters of substantial audiences for their telecasts.

But up-and-coming pay TV moguls such as Levin, who launched HBO and later went on to become the chief executive of AOL Time Warner, were dependent on Johnson to convince Capitol Hill lawmakers to overturn the rules that restricted their right to air the movies. As the industry's point man, Johnson worked closely with these hard-charging entrepreneurs—many of them were on the NCTA board—and he observed every detail of how they were building their businesses. It opened his eyes, as he learned about cable technology, marketing, budgets, and programming. His job put him right at the table where the ideas that would reshape the entire television industry were first batted around. "They're talking bottom line, marketing and everything," Johnson later said. "And I begin to see people who have a business orientation as opposed to a social or political orientation. And it's there where I see the possibility of starting a business."[4]

Hardly a sexy business in those days, cable had already existed for years, but mainly as a means of providing television reception to people in rural backwaters who could not receive decent broadcast signals. But chief executives like Irving Berlin Kahn of TelePrompTer; Chuck Dolan, founder of Cablevision Systems Corporation; and John C. Malone, who took over TeleCommunications Inc. (TCI) in 1972, had recognized its potential and by the mid-1970s their systems were growing rapidly. By 1977, there were 77 million homes with televisions in the United States, and 12 million received cable.[5]

To grow their businesses, these enterprising executives were searching for new original programming ideas to challenge what was being aired on the old broadcast networks, and they were also beginning to compete for the lucrative monopoly rights to install and operate cable systems in the country's major cities. Standing before city councils and planning boards, cable executives made their pitch, and those who could offer the broadest, most diverse programming choices stood a better chance of snagging contracts.

New channels like Home Box Office; Showtime; Ted Turner's TBS Superstation; and the public affairs channel, C-SPAN, were being launched. To the executives building the cable systems, these unique channels were initially not viewed as promising businesses themselves. They were valued mainly as tools to get people to sign up for cable.

Malone, who was quickly turning TCI into the country's largest cable operator, was also serving on the NCTA board at the time. His TCI, which was already operating over 150 systems around the country, had been awarded the franchise contract in Memphis, Tennessee. The city had a large black population, and Malone was eager to find low-cost programming that would attract the city's black residents to install cable in their homes. Moreover, with large black populations centered in other big cities where cable contracts had not yet been awarded, Malone knew that having a channel geared toward blacks could help him win future contracts.

Apparently, none of this escaped Johnson as he went about his duties. He learned that in addition to the needs of the cable operators, there was a neglected audience of black viewers waiting to be tapped. The black population was growing twice as fast as the white population in the United States, and the average number of hours that blacks were spending watching television was much higher. Johnson recalled years later that around this time the idea for a black channel was "in the air." As he told *Billboard* magazine in 2000: "There was this idea that cable would create the kind of diversity that the broadcast networks never had. Someone was going to do it. I was already in the cable industry in the late Seventies. Why not me?"[6]

On one of Malone's visits to Washington for an NCTA meeting, he was approached by Johnson in the lobby of the organization's offices. "Do you think there would be any hope for a channel aimed at the black demographic?" Johnson asked. Malone's face lit up. "I was very enthusiastic," Malone later recalled. "We were trying to build in some markets, heavy black neighborhoods, and we didn't have anything to talk to them about."[7] Once Johnson had a formalized proposal to present, Malone told him, he'd be eager to see it.

Johnson, by all accounts, was doing a good job at the NCTA. The government was inching toward removing regulatory barriers to cable, and the freewheeling entrepreneurs who relied on Johnson's services were recognizing that he was bright and ambitious. Johnson was careful not to appear excessively aggressive and risk offending anyone. His ambition was restrained and carefully measured. People found him easy to like.

One cable entrepreneur with whom Johnson became friendly was Ken Silverman, a former Columbia Pictures executive who had struck out on his own in 1974 and launched Cinemerica, a Beverly Hills, California–based company that focused on developing cable programming. Silverman and Johnson would get together for lunch or dinner in Washington or Los Angeles, or when they were attending industry conventions around the country. Silverman's company was a lean operation with very little funding, and Bob marveled at how the firm managed to make ends meet. "Bob would get a kick out of the way we would do things," recalls Silverman. "We were more entrepreneurial than most."

In 1978, Silverman flew to Washington to enlist Bob's support and assistance in launching a new cable channel that Silverman had created. The channel, Cinemerica Satellite Network, would be targeted at viewers who were age 50 and older. At this time, there were hardly any channels on cable that had narrow, targeted programming. But Silverman had conducted research and found that although the big broadcast networks like CBS, NBC, and ABC were targeting the 50-plus market, those older television viewers weren't buying cable for their homes because the prevailing perception was that cable had theatrical movies that were being made to appeal to children and young adults.

To help push his idea, Silverman needed the NCTA as a cheerleader. At this time, much of the country was still without cable, and as each city went through the hotly contested process of picking an operator to build and operate the local franchise, those that offered the broadest and most appealing programming and services were likely to be chosen. Upon hearing Silverman's plan, Johnson instantly liked the idea for the 50-plus channel and he agreed to help Silverman convince cable operators to include the channel in their lineups.

But what Johnson also quickly recognized was that Silverman had created a road map that could be extended beyond one specific demographic. A couple of months after he first learned of the 50-plus channel, Johnson met again with Silverman in Washington. "You know, I would like to start a black cable network," Johnson informed Silverman, the two men sitting across from each other at Johnson's desk. "How would you feel if I took your business plan, slashed out every reference to 'elderly,' replaced it with 'black,' and changed the numbers accordingly?" A black channel posed no threat to his business, Silverman figured. So without hesitation, he slid a copy of his business plan across the desk. "Take it," he said.[8]

When spring arrived in 1979, the cherry trees in Washington exploded in their annual display of metamorphic splendor, and Robert Johnson, now 33 years old, experienced his own rebirth. His dreams of a life in public service faded, and the capitalist entrepreneur was born. With the outline for a formal

business plan in his hands and a stated interest from an industry heavyweight like John Malone, Johnson had the begin-
nings of a business.

As Johnson started researching the viability of a channel
targeted at blacks, he was assisted by Vivian Goodier, a young
white woman who reported directly to him at the NCTA.
Goodier, a compact brunette who went by the nickname
"Chickie," had joined the NCTA around the same time as
Johnson. They had lobbied together on Capitol Hill and in
the process developed a close relationship. So close, in fact,
that by the time they started working together that summer on
the business plan for the new channel, they were also having a
personal, intimate affair.[9]

If he was to make it on his own, the first thing that Johnson
needed was capital. To beam the signal for his new channel, he
would have to purchase time on satellite transponders, and the
costs would be high. He learned of a firm called Syndicated
Communications Inc. Known as Syncom, it was a new Washing-
ton-based venture fund that was geared toward minority-owned
media and telecommunications. The guy running the firm was
Herbert P. Wilkins, a 36-year-old Boston native who had been a
member of the 1970 class at the Harvard Business School. That
class was especially significant because it marked the first time
that the ultra-elite school had made a concerted effort to diversify beyond its traditional core of white men. Wilkins was one of
about 30 black students in the groundbreaking class.

Johnson telephoned Wilkins, and the two agreed to meet at
Wilkins' office. "He brought the proposal in and I thought it had
a lot of potential," Wilkins recalls. But there was one problem.
Johnson felt he needed about $10 million, and Wilkins' fledgling
firm had total capital of only about $1.75 million. "We walked
away from the deal because we thought we couldn't make a significant enough investment to make it worthwhile," Wilkins says.
But the meeting between the two men kicked off what would

become a vital and enduring partnership. Wilkins, a tall, burly man with a strong New England accent and an intimidating no-nonsense style, would later become an investor in many black-owned businesses, including Johnson's cable channel. Moreover, the two would later team up in other ventures that helped to build Johnson's fortune.

Finding a major cash infusion wasn't easy, but Johnson got a big break that summer while he was working at the annual NCTA show in Las Vegas. The show, which is the industry's biggest gathering each year, provides a forum for developers of shows and channels to present their programming to cable system operators.

On the convention floor that year, Johnson tracked down a man named Bob Rosencrans, who was the chief of a large cable system then known as UA/Columbia Cablevision. UA/Columbia, which ran cable systems in the Northeast, Florida, and Texas, had recently formed a joint venture with the Madison Square Garden in New York City and launched a cable channel. The Madison Square Garden Sports Network, as it was called, showed pretty much all of the events that took place at the Garden, from New York Knicks games to dog shows. The cable companies that carried the channel paid a modest fee per subscriber, and the network sold national advertising slots and gave slots to the local cable company to sell. It was the first cable network to implement this revenue structure, which persisted and became the financial backbone of cable programming. And while premium pay channels like HBO and Showtime were already in existence, the Madison Square Garden Sports Network was the first attempt by the fledgling industry to create an indigenous network with a broad array of programming. Its name was soon changed to USA Network.

The network leased a satellite transponder to beam its programs to cable systems, but with most of the live sports limited to the evening hours it had a lot of valuable unused blocks of time that could be filled with programming. Rosencrans had already provided a block of time in the morning for the launch of the government and public affairs programming known as C-SPAN. Additionally, a block of educational programs aimed at children was shown in the afternoons.

Johnson told Rosencrans about his idea for a channel. "Can you give me two hours on Friday nights for black programming?" Johnson asked. Rosencrans, who wanted to use the network to build more cable subscribers, instantly thought it was a good idea. He reached out and shook Johnson's hand. "Go ahead," he said. "Be our guest."

Rosencrans told Johnson that he could have the two-hour block for free. "It was an enhancement for us because it would bring another market into our group," Rosencrans later recalled. "The essence of cable was to have as much variety as you could." If Johnson had leased his own transponder it would have cost about $300,000 per year; plus he would have needed his own studio facilities to transmit the programming. By using all of the facilities provided by Rosencrans, Johnson lowered his start-up capital needs substantially. Not asking Johnson for a percentage of the equity in his business, Rosencrans now woefully admits, "was the biggest mistake of my life."

With satellite carriage locked up, things began to happen fast. Within a few weeks, on August 8, 1979, Johnson issued a press release announcing the creation of Black Entertainment Television (BET). The network, he promised, would debut the following January. Johnson quit his job, took out a $15,000 loan from a Washington bank, and convinced the NCTA to give him a $15,000 consulting contract for an extra financial cushion. On September 13, he paid $42 to the recorder of deeds in Washington to incorporate BET. According to the document, the company was established with 100 shares valued at $10 each. Its initial board of directors was listed as consisting of three people:

Bob Johnson, a Washington lawyer named Joseph H. Sharlitt, and Sheila Johnson.

Bob Johnson was on his way to earning a fortune. Silverman, who gave Johnson the business plan that became the framework for BET, never got his senior channel off the ground. He never received a penny from Johnson in return for the business plan. And he does not recall ever receiving a "thank you," either.

"WHITE MAN, CAN YOU SPARE HALF A MILLION?"

*If every black entrepreneur had a white John Malone, there would be 200
BETs. There'd be one in the banking business, the airline business, the hotel
business, and the movie business. John got involved in BET, but the money
he invested wasn't the big issue. What he did was put his personal credibility
and prestige into BET, and that's invaluable.*

          —Robert Johnson, *Multichannel News,* 2000

As the jet skidded to a stop at Denver's Stapleton Airport, Bob Johnson prepared for his meeting at the headquarters of the cable power TeleCommunications Incorporated (TCI). He knew that the company's chief executive, John Malone, needed black-oriented programming to broaden his systems and had earlier shown a genuine interest in helping Johnson launch his new channel. But now the moment of truth had arrived. Johnson had to make a formal pitch. What's more, he had to convince Malone to write a check. After all, he had less than two months to go before the scheduled launch of BET.

Malone, a 38-year-old Connecticut native, held degrees in electrical engineering and industrial management from Yale University, New York University, and Johns Hopkins University, where he ultimately received a doctorate. Now he was emerging as one of the shrewdest and most powerful players in the cable business. He had moved out to Denver in 1972 to become chief executive of TCI, a struggling and obscure cable company with less than one million subscribers. And now, just seven years later, Malone had TCI well on its way toward owning 20 percent of the nation's cable households, which would exceed 65 million. Malone himself would eventually have personal control of TCI assets through another company that he would start in 1991, Liberty Media.

In fact, Malone would eventually reign so completely over the industry that his success would become an obsession among government antitrust regulators and he would disparagingly be labeled the "Darth Vader" of the cable business. One of the first steps he took toward broadening his power was when he agreed to the meeting with Johnson. At the time, Malone was just beginning to realize that with cable's rapid growth, he could enjoy far greater success if he not only owned the distribution systems, but also had a stake in the content itself. Programmers such as the budding MTV video music channel were just starting to push for subscriber fees from cable operators. Up until then, cable channels, like their broadcast brethren, were dependent on advertising sales as their sole source of revenue. If Malone could find some promising programming ideas to invest in, then TCI could position itself to benefit from the dual revenue stream that cable programmers were sure to enjoy in the future.

So when Johnson arrived at Malone's office on that November day in 1979, the TCI chief was keenly interested in what this aggressive young black entrepreneur had up his sleeve. So interested, in fact, that when Johnson handed over his business plan,

Malone almost instantly gave his verdict. "How much do you need?" he asked, startling Johnson.

But Johnson displayed the calm under pressure that would become his trademark. He explained to Malone that his budget called for a half million dollars to get BET off the ground. "Okay, Bob, here's what I'll do," Malone said, setting up his pitch. "I will buy 20 percent of your company for $180,000, and I'll loan you $320,000. I'll have 20 percent and you'll have 80 percent. Is that a deal?"[1]

He tried not to let on, but Johnson thought it all sounded too good to be true. He would later confide that even if Malone had reversed the numbers and taken 80 percent of the company and left him with 20 percent, he would have gone along with the deal. "What he didn't know is that I would have taken the 20 percent," Johnson later said. "But John said he thought I'd work harder for myself than for him."[2]

Within minutes, Malone's lawyer was in the office drafting an agreement. The five-page letter of agreement signed by both men on November 12, 1979, outlines the deal. Malone would immediately pay Johnson the $180,000 for the equity stake. The remaining loan would work like a line of credit. For a period of one year, BET could draw down as much as $30,000 per month. The loan would carry an interest rate of 6 percent annually and for a five-year period Johnson had the right to convert the outstanding principal and interest into BET stock, increasing TCI's equity in his company up to as much as 33⅓ percent. If he did not convert the debt to equity, the loan had to be paid in full within five years. And until it was fully repaid, Johnson was required to make one-third of all of his excess operating cash—the money left over after he covered his operating expenses—available to TCI for repayment of the loan.

The letter of agreement went on to clarify a host of issues. TCI would have representation on BET's board, and Johnson would be required to seek approval from Malone on major financial matters. Johnson, however, would have "full operating control" of the company, assuming all responsibility for programming, production, advertising, and day-to-day matters. But Malone—like all the white cable operators who at the time were itching to diversify their programming as a means of attracting more cable subscribers—was also a little nervous about what he was getting himself into. He worried about what this so-called black-oriented programming would actually look like. Malone was a well-educated man, but he did not know much about black taste and culture. What would a channel like BET actually put on the air?

"There was always this concern that this kind of channel could become radical and you wouldn't want your name associated with it," Malone would later recall. But "Bob seemed like the kind of guy that you could invest some money with and he wouldn't embarrass you."[3]

He may have felt relatively comfortable with Johnson, but Malone still wanted to protect his own image and that of his company. To that end, the agreement letter made it clear that TCI would not be liable for any claims arising from BET's programming selection. Also, Malone included a couple of lines in the agreement that must have seemed routine then, but years later read as if he was prescient in anticipating the future controversy that BET would encounter. The letter stated: "All programming shall conform to the ordinary standards of good taste and decency prevailing in the communities in which BET exhibits."

Within about 45 minutes after first sitting down with Malone, Johnson received TCI's check paying for the 20 percent stake in his company. As he was about to leave Malone's office, he had a harrowing thought. "I've never run a business," he said to Malone. "What advice can you give me?" Malone was blunt: "Get your revenues up, and keep your costs down." It was a tenet that Johnson would live by.[4]

Flying back to D.C., Johnson tried to concentrate on preparations for BET's launch. It wasn't easy to focus, however, because he still could not believe that he now had the most difficult piece of the entrepreneurial puzzle in place: seed capital. "I was nervous," Johnson later admitted. "I got that check and that was more money than I had ever seen in my life. I figured the plane was going to crash on the way back. Something had to happen."[5]

The partnership that he struck that day with Malone would flourish and prove invaluable. BET was TCI's first investment in programming, and Malone went on to invest TCI's money in more than 30 other programming ventures, from the Discovery channel to American Movie Classics and the QVC shopping channel. Yet BET would prove to be one of Malone's most lucrative moves. And as Johnson's channel would grow, Malone would become his quiet mentor, rarely making his presence felt within BET, but at the same time providing Johnson with critical guidance, especially on matters involving financial markets, and debt and equity structure. Malone would hold on to TCI's stake in BET until the very end. The two men, five years apart in age and quite different in many ways, enjoyed a great business relationship but never really became friends socially. It was a relationship that would be built on one thing: a mutual interest in making money.

"It's just rare that white men and black men come together on an eye-to-eye basis," Johnson says. "My relationship with John Malone is strictly business. I've known him for 21 years. I've been in his house all of four times. Yet I've made more money with him than with anybody."[6]

Once he returned to Washington, Johnson began preparing for BET's launch. Three of the country's largest cable system operators, Warner Cable, TelePrompTer, and American Telecommunications Corporation, had already agreed to carry BET on their systems, so with distribution in place, what Johnson now needed was staff to help get things going. By now, he was so convinced of the viability of his business that he could also sell others on it. He talked two of his colleagues at the NCTA into joining him in his new venture. One was his secretary at the agency, Carol E. Coody. The other was Vivian "Chickie" Goodier, the NCTA executive with whom he had been working closely and having an intimate affair.

Already, Johnson was displaying one key quality that great business leaders possess: charisma. It was like the scene from the Tom Cruise movie, *Jerry Maguire*, where the main character packs up his belongings in his office, heads for the door, and with all of his colleagues watching asks: "Who's coming with me?" In Bob's case, Goodier and Coody answered the call.

Coody agreed to serve as BET's "special assistant" handling all administrative and secretarial chores for a salary of $14,000. Goodier was paid about $40,000 to become vice president for affiliate relations, in charge of securing agreements with cable system operators to carry BET. To reward them for taking the risk and becoming his first employees, Johnson promised that he would later give them a nonvoting equity stake in BET, making them not just workers but partial owners also. Their "beneficial interest" shares would be equal to the value of BET stock, but Johnson's agreement with Malone required that Johnson himself keep voting control of the shares.

Johnson made the same promise to his next hire, his older sister Paulette. Known as Polly, she was close to her brother and because she had done some bookkeeping in the past, Johnson figured she was the perfect person to trust with BET's financial records. For a salary of $25,000, Polly Johnson agreed to leave her home in Waukegan, Illinois, and relocate to Washington to work for her brother as BET's comptroller. Johnson rented a small, three-room office in the prestigious Georgetown section of Washington, and BET's inaugural workforce of four went to work.

What the three women in the office soon realized was that

they had signed on to work with a man who never rested, and did not expect them to rest, either. With BET's scheduled launch only weeks away, Johnson worked to secure the rights to the old Negro films that would comprise BET's early programming and to sign up advertisers. Johnson and his staff worked long, hard hours each day. It began to pay off on January 21, 1980, just four days before BET was scheduled to premiere, when Johnson secured his first slate of advertisers. Six national companies became the network's charter sponsors: Anheuser-Busch, Time, Champale, Pepsi-Cola, Sears, and Kellogg.

Black Entertainment Television was ready to sign on for the first time. But first, Johnson and his colleagues had one small problem to solve. Washington, D.C., like many big cities, was not even wired for cable yet, so the BET staff had to find a place where they themselves could view the historic telecast. They located a small facility out in northern Virginia that had cable and received the USA Network, the channel that had agreed to give BET its two-hour block on Friday nights.

The BET launch party was a humble affair. There were drinks and light snacks. The main course was one of Johnson's favorite potato chips. A total of about 10 people attended, and since the entire block of programming was taped and shipped off to USA Network, there were no chores for BET's staff to perform that night. Before the network debuted at 11 P.M., Johnson spoke briefly, quoting the legendary CBS network pioneer, William S. Paley. "It was kind of funny," recalled Virgil Hemphill, Johnson's college fraternity brother, who flew in from Chicago for the occasion. "No one was taking BET seriously yet, but he had the nerve to be quoting William Paley."

The first program to show on BET was the movie *A Visit to a Chief's Son*. The 1974 adventure, starring the longtime character actor Richard Mulligan, is about a father and his teenage son who draw closer together when they travel to Africa to study the rituals of the Masai tribe. "It was uplifting and pro-social," Johnson later said. "The right kind of thing for us in the early days."[7] BET, the first-ever black-oriented television outlet, was officially on the air, reaching 3.8 million subscribers in 350 markets across the country. Everyone at the party watched the entire BET programming block that night, proudly inspecting every single commercial break and station identification. "It wasn't a big thing, but it felt very important," Hemphill recalled. "It felt like an important step in communications."

Hemphill, who had worked in production at the local CBS affiliate in Chicago and was teaching college courses at the time, obtained a leave from his job and took charge of producing BET's programming. Early on, the job consisted primarily of putting the movies onto videotapes and inserting the commercial spots. He would send the tapes to the USA Network production office, and technicians there would pop them in on Friday night and uplink to the satellite. Hemphill, however, did not want to move his family to Washington, so for about two years he did the job from Chicago.

Johnson was hands-on in every area of the business. He even conducted some of the network's first on-air interviews, and for a broadcasting neophyte, he was remarkably comfortable in front of the camera. But more than anything, Johnson was a salesman. Most advertisers still had no regard for the market that BET was attempting to build, and most people did not think that this little black-owned cable company had much of a chance of surviving. But Johnson crisscrossed the country with the zeal of an evangelist, calling on advertising agencies, cable operators, and just about anyone who could help the network to grow and flourish.

Much of the ad spending aimed at the black market was managed by the small number of black-owned agencies, and Johnson quickly made himself acquainted with those people. He would travel to Chicago and meet with Barbara Proctor of Proctor and Gardner. While there, he'd pay a visit to Thomas J. Burrell of Burrell Communications. And before returning to

Washington, he'd stop in New York to call on Byron Lewis of Uniworld Advertising. He would sometimes take Virgil or Chickie along on these trips for support and so that the agency heads could meet other executives and see that BET was a real company, not just a one-man show. Johnson would show a sample tape of the programming and lay out his vision for how the network would expand its subscriber base. He used whatever statistics he could find to prove the economic viability of the market that he was trying to serve. Instead of the television advertising that was produced for the general market using mostly white actors, Johnson needed advertising geared toward his audience, he explained.

The black-owned agencies liked what they heard. But their clients, the big consumer products companies, fast-food restaurants, and auto manufacturers, had never spent any money on black-targeted television. Other than a few syndicated television shows like *Soul Train* and *Don Kushner's Rock Concert*, advertising produced for and aimed at blacks was limited to magazines like *Ebony*, *Jet*, and *Essence*. "We tried real hard," recalls Lewis. But "our clients were not prepared to spend the money to be on the network."

But no resistance or rejection seemed to discourage Johnson. Instead, he became more intense and more single-minded in his focus. While many people stood by doubting that his company would survive for even a year or two, he remained at full throttle. A tireless promoter of his new venture, Johnson constantly preached the virtues of BET to just about anyone who would listen. As one associate recalls: "He was obsessed. People would run when they saw him coming."

It would take years, but as the network grew in size and in reputation, the advertising followed. And along with the ad dollars that would flow into BET, the black-owned agencies would also flourish as a result of the network. Companies expanded their television advertising budgets, for the first time making allowances for black-targeted commercials. The black-owned agencies grew, most of them producing television campaigns for the first time. Eventually, in fact, they became so successful that they either merged with or were bought out by large mainstream ad agencies that decided that they, too, wanted to be in the business of creating black-targeted advertising.

Five months after launching the channel, Johnson made his first big programming move. He allocated $1 million toward producing and airing football and basketball games played at predominantly black colleges. These schools had educated a large percentage of his target market and they had sent many athletes into the pro ranks, yet other than the occasional game played by a powerhouse like Grambling State, their teams rarely appeared on national television. BET filled the void.

But with a tight budget and just four employees, producing the games was not easy in the early days. Hemphill, who was still based in Chicago, would scout the location of the game in advance, hire production crews and announcers, and lease the big mobile studio trucks used for telecasting from remote sites. It was a heavy load for one person, so Johnson one day suggested that his assistant, Carol, accompany Hemphill to set up the productions.

But with most of the black colleges located throughout the South, Hemphill did not think it would be a good idea for him to travel alone with a young white woman. "Carol was a hard-working, smart young lady," says Hemphill, a tall, brown, bearish man. "But I didn't think the two of us should travel together down South." Johnson understood Hemphill's concern. So instead of Carol, Johnson assigned his sister, Polly, to help out with the games. And Johnson himself would also travel to each game, conducting on-air interviews with the college presidents during halftime. "He got accustomed to working with television," Hemphill says. "He was comfortable with being on camera."

Off camera, though, Johnson and Polly would often get into arguments. Although he trusted his sister with the financial books, they would bicker like an old married couple. Polly seemed to especially like public drama. She'd wait until they were all rushing around at the motel, about to head over to the stadium, and then she'd "go ape shit," recalls Hemphill. "She'd be mad at Bobby about something back at the office, and the argument would escalate."

Johnson counted heavily on Chickie Goodier to assist with most aspects of the business. She accompanied Johnson to cable trade shows, where they pitched BET to cable system operators. For BET's first National Cable Television Association convention, the trade group that they both had worked for, Johnson and Goodier purchased a booth. Amid the lavish, expensive exhibits that big cable channels had constructed on the convention floor, BET set up a small card table with handmade signs. Johnson, Hemphill, and Goodier stood by proudly, introducing convention delegates to their new channel.

Goodier would also follow up on sales calls that Johnson had made, and she would assume responsibility in the office whenever he was out. A thin, dark-haired woman in her late twenties, Goodier put in long hours to help get BET off the ground, and the others at the office—who were also working extremely hard—could see that Goodier and Johnson seemed to have a special rapport. Soon, they began to suspect that there might be more than business to the relationship between Johnson and Goodier.

While his wife Sheila was busy teaching music at the elite Sidwell Friends School and giving violin lessons on the side, Johnson was working late most nights. Even when he and the staff took a break for dinner, it was a work-related dinner. Yet as hard as they all worked, they were always overloaded, as there was simply too much work for just five people. Johnson was adamant about running BET like a real business. He insisted that all paperwork such as contracts, billings, or receipts was properly handled. And even though the staff was small, he made his employees adhere to a corporate structure, which meant that everyone except Johnson had to report to Chickie. It did not help matters that the others were growing suspicious of the personal relationship between Chickie and Johnson. According to staffers, Polly and Chickie often got into arguments. Inside the Georgetown office, the tension hung in the air like fumes from an old leaky gas oven, waiting for some unlucky soul to strike a match.

One day, Johnson decided he had had enough of the constant bickering. He telephoned Hemphill in Chicago. "You better get here," Johnson urged Hemphill. "I can't take it anymore. I'm about to fire all of them." Hemphill jumped on a flight to Washington. He arrived at the office to find his colleagues arguing over who was in charge of what. Agreeing to all sit down and sort it out, they diffused a potential disaster, and got back to work.[8]

But the tension did not abate. Johnson would grow frustrated that his sister lacked the type of polish that he had gained in college and in Washington. As he saw it, she was far too emotional and unable to accept her younger brother's authority. Polly knew what many others would also learn over the years: Behind the calm, smiling exterior, Johnson could be cold and callous. She complained that he was bent on controlling her. "If I didn't do exactly what he wanted me to do," she said, "if I wasn't exactly like him, he was going to come back and tell me that I was crazy, or I had a problem, or I didn't like white people, or he was going to demean me in some kind of way."[9] In a 1992 deposition, she accused her brother of being "evil" and of even trying to turn their own mother against her.

The intense sibling rivalry was only aggravated by the sexual tension between Johnson and his second-in-command, Goodier. Finally, the two decided that their personal relationship was interfering with business. They agreed her voluntary resignation would be in the best interest of the company. In late 1982, Goodier left BET. She took a job in New York at the Disney Channel. It was not, however, the last that Johnson would hear from her.

Meanwhile, Polly Johnson remained with BET, fussing and fighting incessantly with her brother. But she would soon become far more than a mere nuisance. She was about to cause BET's first corporate scandal.

REVEREND ELDORADO

Riding along the interstate, heading to Rehoboth Beach, Delaware, for a couple of days of much-needed rest, Bob Johnson was feeling particularly good about how things were going with his business and his life as a mogul in the making. Over in the passenger seat was his new friend, the television actor Tim Reid, who had become famous as the disc jockey known as Venus Flytrap on the hit 1978 sitcom, *WKRP in Cincinnati*. It was the mid-1980s, and the business world had recently been shocked when a black Harvard-trained lawyer and investment banker, Reginald Lewis, shot to fast fame and enormous wealth with his $1 billion leveraged buyout of the food company Beatrice International.

Few black businesspeople had ever imagined reaching the level of wealth that Lewis had achieved. But Johnson was imagining it—and much more. Glancing away from the road and over at Reid, Johnson told his friend: "I'm going to be rich. I want to be the first black billionaire."[1] Reid could not believe what he was hearing. He knew that BET had great potential, but he was sure that Johnson's expectations were exceeding reality. "I was making 10 times what he was making, and he was saying that he was going to be a billionaire," Reid later recalled. "I looked at him and thought, 'In what dream?'"

Reid had good reason to be skeptical.

By 1982, the man who would become the nation's first black billionaire was earning just $65,000 a year as BET's chief executive officer. He was spending much of his time on the road, meeting with advertisers and the hundreds of cable system operators spread around the country. "Bob got to know every cable operator personally," says his friend and business partner, Herb Wilkins. "He made it his business to know them all." And as Virgil Hemphill, BET's first production head, put it, "Bob was his best salesman. He was the deal closer."

The network was still not making a profit, but the hard work appeared to be paying off. The list of major advertisers had grown to include General Electric, Xerox, Amtrak, and Mobil Oil, and the network was now received by 8 million subscribers in over 500 cable markets. But BET was still on the air only one night per week, a four-hour block late on Friday evenings. It was getting so little exposure that many viewers weren't even sure whether BET was an actual network or just a weekly television show. It needed a much larger presence, which would require additional funding.

Johnson raised more money by selling a 20 percent interest in BET to Taft Broadcasting Company in exchange for $1 million. Taft, which later became the Great American Broadcasting Company, owned WDCA-TV, a local independent television station in Washington. Through the partnership, BET was able to rent WDCA's studio facilities to produce shows.

Johnson negotiated to lease six hours a day, seven days a week on a new satellite transponder. Although the new transponder would provide many more hours of exposure, a large number of his current subscribers were on cable systems that did not receive the signal from the new satellite. Consequently, as a result of making the switch and gaining more viewing hours, BET lost 6 million, or three-fourths, of its subscribers. It would prove to be a wise sacrifice, as the expanded schedule would make the network much more attractive to ad buyers and cable operators.

With all of the additional airtime, Johnson now had to come up with a lot more programming to fill the schedule. He had already added a couple of half-hour shows to his lineup, most notably *The Bobby Jones Gospel Show*. It was an "off-network" production, which meant the program was produced outside BET, which then bought the rights to air it. The weekly songfest eventually made Jones, a former elementary school teacher who wears custom-made, bright-colored suits with gold buttons and sparkling adornments, one of the most important people in the world of gospel music. The show was still on the network more than 20 years later.

Just as he had done with black college sports, Johnson used the gospel program to provide entertainment that he knew black people enjoyed but rarely saw anywhere else on television. Many blacks had gained their musical foundations in churches, and although some radio stations devoted Sunday mornings to gospel, no television shows were devoted to the musical genre. Moreover, Johnson acquired the shows on the cheap.

Johnson could see, early on, that he could serve large numbers of viewers with low-budget fare. The key was to choose programs that a broad market could relate to. When choosing which football games to air, for example, he avoided the smaller, lesser-known black colleges and focused instead on the ones with national popularity, such as Jackson State and Grambling. And he made sure he selected schools that had good marching bands, because some of the bands, such as the one at Florida A&M—with their high-stepping style and flashy showmanship—were legendary in the black community. For BET, the half-time band performances were a bonus: exclusive entertainment for the network. And it all came at a low price. For the broadcast rights to each game, BET paid about $500 to each school. By comparison, the big broadcast networks at that time were paying as much as $50,000 for major college football games. Including expenses for talent and crew, BET produced the games for less than $15,000 each.

On some occasions, after BET had programmed its six hours there would still be 10 to 15 minutes of empty space to fill on the program reel. BET found the perfect filler. Record labels had made promotional tapes of artists to use for marketing purposes, allowing record store owners or distributors to get a look at the artists. The tapes usually showed the artist performing a song or two, and the production quality was not very good, as the tapes were typically shot using a couple of cameras and very little in the way of special effects. Among the tapes that had been produced at the time were productions by the group Shalamar singing "A Night to Remember," Lakeside's "Fantastic Voyage," and the fast-paced hit "And the Beat Goes On," by the crooners known as The Whispers. Such promotional tapes were the only black videos around at the time. The music video channel MTV had just been launched and was quickly growing popular. However, MTV's format was exclusively rock and pop. It totally ignored rhythm and blues, the genre most popular among black people at the time.

Johnson and Hemphill found someone who could get the promotional videos from the record labels. Figuring it was an easy way for the artists to get exposure, the middleman let BET use the videos for free. Eventually, BET started dealing directly with the record labels, who continued to provide the tapes free of charge. With MTV leaving a huge void in the fledgling video music scene, Johnson sensed an opportunity. "When MTV started they didn't play black music," Johnson recalled years later. "So they opened that door for us."

In 1981, BET launched its first music program, *Video Soul,* a half-hour show devoted to black recording artists. At the beginning, it was a low-cost, crude production. MTV, when it launched, had conducted a national search for what it termed "video disc jockeys," the on-air personalities who would do in-studio introductions of the videos. However, when it was time for Hemphill to find talent for *Video Soul*, he did not search far. He hired one local Chicago radio personality, LaDonna Tittle, to do some part-time on-air work. However, the star of the show was a character that Hemphill created, and he himself played. Dressing in a big hat and flashy suit, Hemphill dubbed himself Reverend Eldorado. It was a takeoff of the parodies of showy, black Southern preachers that comics like Richard Pryor were popularizing at the time. The good Reverend Eldorado, speaking in an exaggerated, rhythmic style, would introduce the videos. "*Video Soul* initially cost very little," recalls Hemphill. "I was real cheap talent."

Building on the foundation that was now in place, Johnson began to take major steps toward strategic growth. He moved the company to a larger office in the Georgetown neighborhood, and made a string of key hires. He staffed BET, from top to bottom, with young, ambitious African-Americans, many of them graduates of communications programs at black colleges like Howard University in Washington and Hampton University, located three hours south in Virginia. The pay that he offered was not great, but the opportunity was enormous, as many of these young people assumed far more responsibility than they were likely to ever have at a mainstream company.

In 1982, Johnson brought on Janis Thomas, a 27-year-old who had been working in advertising trafficking at a local TV station, as his first vice president of advertising services.

And with the move to a six-hour, seven-day-a-week schedule and the need to ramp up production, he hired Jefferi Lee, a 25-year-old production employee at the CBS affiliate in Washington. Hemphill was still in Chicago and unwilling to relocate to Washington. Consequently, Lee, as program and operations manager, took over Hemphill's programming responsibilities. After allowing Hemphill to continue to produce some shows under contract, Johnson decided he no longer could use the services of his old college buddy, and fired him. "Never in my wildest dreams did I think BET would be as big as it ended up being," Hemphill said years later after he became a college professor in Chicago. Shortly after Lee joined BET he was promoted to vice president of network operations, and many years later he became president and chief operating officer of the company.

One of Lee's first duties at BET was to expand the music programming from the weekly half-hour *Video Soul* to six hours a week. The new show was produced in Washington, and in addition to video clips it included interviews with artists and behind-the-scenes accounts of the music industry. To host the show, Lee hired a popular Washington disc jockey, Donnie Simpson, and a lovely, fresh-faced newcomer, Sheila Banks. Also, to help fill the six-hour daily block, Lee purchased the rights to air old black films, such as the musical *Stormy Weather* starring Lena Horne, as well as more modern fare like the Diana Ross classic, *Lady Sings the Blues*. But by the time that Lee had the six-hour schedule full, Johnson told him to get ready to go to a 24-hour schedule.

The boss was eager to grow. He struck a deal with Home Box Office (HBO), the movie channel that cable customers received only if they paid an extra premium to their cable operators. HBO, owned by media giant Time Inc., had available satellite transponder space. To become a 24-hour operation, BET needed the additional satellite capacity. In exchange for access to the transponder, Johnson gave HBO a 15 percent equity stake in BET. The transponder space was worth about $2 million to $3 million annually, so within a year the deal reached parity and BET began paying for the access to the transponder. But now that he was a partner with two of the biggest cable operators in the country, TCI and Time Inc., Johnson had tremendous leverage to sell his channel to advertisers and other cable systems.

A short while later, Johnson asked his new partners for additional assistance. He called Don Anderson, who at the time was building HBO's operations on the West Coast. "Look, I need help,"[2] Johnson told Anderson. Other than himself, Johnson had no staff to sell the channel to cable operators, and his small, struggling company was in dire need of expertise in several areas.

Anderson, who was now one of Time Inc.'s top African-American executives, began working on an arrangement that called for him to manage the marketing and affiliate sales for BET. He would use a small staff comprised of HBO employees, and BET would pay a fee of about $450,000 annually for the marketing and sales assistance. "They were fledgling, limited and inferior," says Anderson. "But they had a good concept with programming aimed at this subset of the population."

But inside Time Inc., there was some trepidation among executives about whether it made sense to become so deeply involved with BET. The company had a history of lending support to fledgling black-owned firms such as *Essence* magazine and the Mutual Black Radio Network, but not everyone was on board in this case. When he was tapped to oversee the BET investment, Anderson left the West Coast and returned to New York. Nicholas J. Nicholas Jr., who was chief financial officer at the time, called him to his office. Known within the company as Mahogany Row for its expensive wood paneling, the 32nd floor of the Time-Life Building in midtown Manhattan was where all of the top executives were housed. Upon his arrival on Mahogany Row, Anderson was told by Nicholas that Michael Fuchs, who had just been made head of the HBO unit, did not think that the BET investment was a worthwhile use of resources. Nicholas assured Anderson that he supported the deal, but warned him: "Stay out of Mike's way."

A few days later, while he was still waiting for final approval from the Time Inc. board, Anderson received a phone call from Fuchs. "I need to see you right away," Fuchs told him. When Anderson arrived at Fuchs' office, the HBO chief was his normal blunt self. "I don't think we ought to do the BET deal," Fuchs said. Anderson, knowing that he had the backing of Nicholas, refuted the authority of his new boss. "I don't think you have anything to do with this," he told Fuchs. "It's not in your hands." The short, terse meeting ended abruptly. Anderson went back and informed Nicholas of the encounter with Fuchs. Nicholas reassured him. "Lie low," Nicholas said. "I'll take care of it."

Within days, the Time Inc. board approved the deal, and Johnson and Anderson were posing for photos together as they signed the agreement. Anderson used HBO's resources to help BET develop a rate card, allowing the network to begin charging cable affiliates a fee per subscriber to carry BET on their systems. HBO's engineering department helped BET's engineers develop their technical skills. A black lawyer from Time Inc.'s legal department, Robert Gerard, helped BET with the contracts that it signed with cable systems. "Bob was lucky that there were just enough blacks in strategic positions at the company to help BET get started," says Anderson.

Over the next three years, Anderson and his group more than doubled BET's subscriber base to nearly 18 million viewers. Now the network had two revenue streams. In addition to advertising dollars, BET was also receiving one to two cents per subscriber each month from cable operators. "We grew the business," Anderson said years later. "I admire what Bob has accomplished, but there are a lot of people who Bob never said 'thank you' to."

With its move to 24 hours per day of programming, BET's staff doubled overnight to about 40 people. The company was now split between two locations: Executives and support staff were housed at the Georgetown office, inside the American Trial Lawyers building, and the production staff was in Bethesda, Maryland, inside a small office at a WDCA-TV facility, a former office supply store that the Taft-owned station had transformed into a studio.

For the most part, Johnson now stayed away from production, leaving it in Lee's hands. The running joke around the office was that Johnson had little interest in the quirks and demands of the creative types. "I don't understand you production people," he'd dismissively quip. "That's Jeff's area."[3]

But on the first day that the network signed on for 24-hour telecasting, October 1, 1984, Johnson made a rare appearance at the production office. Addressing the troops inside their cramped quarters, his words were simple, yet lofty as usual. "Our goal," he told the staff, "is to make BET the predominant source for advertisers to reach the black consumer."[4] Life at BET was truly entrepreneurial. The entire production department was based inside one room. There were a few desks for the staff of BET News, which in 1986 debuted as the first national news program aimed at African-Americans. There were a few desks for public affairs, and a few for sports. There were no dividers between any of the desks or departments because the room was too small to fit them in.

Most of the young staffers were recently out of college and had little work experience. "There were no rules," said Alvin Jones, a producer and host of *Video Vibrations*, one of channel's ever-expanding lineup of music video shows. "Everybody was fresh in concept but had no actual experience. You learned as you went along." But, as Johnson insisted, the young workers learned the basics of working for a corporation. They filled out purchase orders, travel authorization forms, and invoices. "We learned the whole nine yards," Jones says. "We learned that there was a process for getting things done, and I'm sure it went on inside other businesses. But for me, it was my first time."

There were mistakes made by the young professionals. And when it's television, mistakes are often viewed by many. Because BET shared studio and video machinery with the independent broadcaster WDCA, there were times when programs got mixed up. On a Saturday morning, for example, BET would come back from a commercial break and a control room engineer would switch to the wrong tape machine. Instead of seeing BET's scheduled program, a WDCA cartoon such as *Scooby-Do* would appear on BET.

The network's music video library was a small supply closet. It housed all videos. By now, BET's presence was starting to create a greater demand for black videos, but the supply was still limited. When *Video Vibrations* debuted, the very first video that aired was "When Doves Cry," by Prince, who at the time was rising to become a superstar in the industry. Other hot videos of the era were "Girl I Want Your Body," by the Jacksons, and "Jungle Love," by Morris Day and The Time. But the limited supply of videos by black artists forced BET to tap into the much larger supply of available videos featuring white artists. The network played songs like Bruce Springstein's "Born in the USA," and others from artists such as David Bowie and Mick Jagger—the types whose music had a soulful, crossover appeal.

Jeff Lee went directly to the record labels and asked them to produce more videos in exchange for a guaranteed amount of exposure each day. The labels, however, were slow to respond, clearly underestimating the valuable promotional outlet that BET was becoming. In 1983, when the Rick James and Smokey Robinson collaboration, "Ebony Eyes" was produced on video by Berry Gordy Jr., the cost was $70,000. It was a breakthrough, as no one had been known before then to make such a financial commitment to a black music video. It had taken so long to produce the "Ebony Eyes" video that by the time it came out the song was no longer on the charts. "But we didn't care," Jones recalls. "It was a black video, it was seven minutes long, and we were like, 'Let's play it.'"[5]

Slowly, the tiny world inside BET's production office and studio became an important place in the music industry. Stars began to make a point of coming by to do on-air interviews and discuss their latest releases. And for many of them, BET was the first place that provided such opportunities. On one occasion a pretty, rising young singer named Whitney Houston stopped by to debut a new video for her 1985 single "You Give Good Love." Before going on the air to chat with Donnie Simpson, she sat in a small conference room that was used as a greenroom. Wearing a scarf on her head and sunglasses, Houston appeared timid and shy—offering no hint of the troubled diva that was in the making. Lee looked into the room and remarked to a colleague: "She's in there looking as quiet as a church mouse."[6]

Back at BET's headquarters, a bombshell was exploding. An anonymous letter dated July 12, 1985, was received by Johnson's partner, TCI chief John Malone. The letter read:

I regret that I am the one who must inform you of the unlawful act of embezzlement that has been carried out by one of Black Entertainment Television's highest-ranking employees.

It has come to my attention that Ms. Paulette Johnson, Vice President for Finance and sister to the president of the company, has embezzled funds from BET thru [sic] the use of her assigned company American Express card. Ms. Johnson has used her card for the purchase of personal items to the tune of over $28,000 between the period of October 1983 and April 1985 without any attempt to reimburse the company prior to being caught. Ms. Johnson was "caught" and her charges verified with the American Express Company thru an outside auditor [Frank Benson, formerly of Seidman and Seidman Accountants]. She was not terminated. Instead, she was given the proverbial "tap on the wrist." This incident is being kept quiet only because she is the president's "sister." Anyone else would have been terminated immediately or prosecuted. However, despite their kinship, I believe this situation warrants your attention. After all, you are an equity partner [16%] in BET. It is my opinion that the partners involved in BET would not want such a person handling the finances of a company they have invested heavily in. Therefore, I feel it is my duty to inform you of such an unsavory deed, thereby allowing you to protect your investment.

The letter goes on to reveal that Paulette Johnson had, after being caught, signed a promissory note to repay the money. And then at the end, the letter writer reveals a mutinous spirit by telling Malone that if he calls a meeting of all BET employees at the company's headquarters, then at that time "I am prepared to come forth and identify myself."

Malone took the letter and passed it on to his secretary with a note that read, "Ask Bob for explanation." Johnson got back to Malone, explaining that the letter was accurate and that he was "embarrassed that this was his sister."[7] He said he "was working it out" and "she would probably be terminated." That was good enough for Malone, who did not dabble in BET's operational affairs. "As far as I was concerned," Malone later said in his deposition, the issues with Paulette "were taken care of."

But Johnson now was faced with a difficult decision. Friends say that despite the constant bickering and tension between the siblings, Johnson clearly loved his sister and wanted her to succeed. But now the pressure was building. Anderson, over at HBO, also received a copy of the letter. He made a point of keeping it from Fuchs, fearing that it would surely kill the partnership. Immediately, Anderson contacted Johnson. "You've got to get rid of your sister," he told him.

Both Paulette Johnson and Carol Coody had by now grown unhappy at BET. Coody, who had been promoted to vice president of communications, was burned out and suffering from exhaustion, which led to a rash of health-related absences from work. Paulette, meanwhile, was struggling to deal with emotional problems as well as the embezzlement revelations. As the only original BET employees other than Johnson himself left at the company, both women were feeling pushed aside by the steady influx of new colleagues arriving on a regular basis. "They had worked nonstop since BET started," says Robin Beamon, who was Coody's assistant. "They had worked like dogs."[8]

Paulette, in fact, seemed at times to be growing despondent. She talked forlornly about "trying to find a reason to live,"[9] and Johnson had in fact contacted family members back in Freeport informing them that she was in trouble. At one time, he even offered to pay for any of them to come visit Paulette in Washington. Eventually, Johnson wrote a letter to Paulette, telling her not to come back to BET. She also was told that he had changed the lock on the door to her office.

But Paulette refused to be fired. She met with her brother and told him that she was quitting and that she wanted her vacation pay, severance pay, and personal files. According to Paulette, her brother's response was chilling. "Bitch, you will get nothing from me until you crawl," he told her.[10]

In November 1985, Paulette Johnson officially left BET. A month later, Coody was also out. Both women said they resigned. Johnson, however, would later contend that they were fired.

COUNTRY BOY CHARM, PREDATOR'S HEART

D on Anderson answered the telephone in his New York office, and on the line was the man known as the godfather of black business. It was the late 1980s. And to Anderson, who was now a senior vice president at Time Inc. and one of the highest-ranking African-Americans in the media business, the mellow, seasoned voice on the other end of the phone sounded familiar.

It was John H. Johnson (no relation to Bob Johnson), the chairman and founder of Johnson Publishing Company, the Chicago-based publisher of *Ebony* and *Jet* magazines. John Harold Johnson had launched his company more than 40 years earlier, thanks to a $500 loan from his mother. But now his firm, which included Fashion Fair Cosmetics, the *Ebony* Fashion Fair traveling fashion show, and a book publishing unit, was grossing $240 million annually and for years had been the largest black-owned company in the country. But John Johnson was sensing that there was an alarm at the gate.

"You're not playing fair," he sternly told Anderson. A little stunned by the admonishment, Anderson listened as Johnson went on to explain that BET was competing for the same advertising dollars as *Ebony*, *Jet*, and other black-owned publications such as *Black Enterprise* and *Essence* magazines. But with financing coming from media titans like TCI and HBO, John Johnson said, BET had an unfair advantage. "BET is not minority-owned," the *Ebony* founder shouted. "It's a white company."[1]

As he had done before when other people made similar allegations, Anderson acknowledged that Time Inc.'s HBO and other mainstream companies had indeed taken minority stakes in BET in exchange for funding. However, he told John Johnson, "BET is majority-owned by a black man."[2] But what John Johnson saw as unfair was the fact that Bob Johnson had been able to keep BET operating during those early lean years by borrowing additional money from his partners. To make interest payments on those loans, which totaled about $8 million, Bob sold the partners additional shares in BET. However, instead of watering down his own equity stake, he increased the total number of shares outstanding and gave each partner additional stock. By 1989, Bob Johnson held 51.3 percent of BET, Malone's TCI held 25.3 percent in partnership with Great American Broadcasting, Time Inc.'s HBO held 16.6 percent, and TCI held an additional 6.6 percent by itself.

Still, to John Johnson, who was now in his seventies and had built his company without ever ceding any of the ownership or control to anyone outside of his family, the kind of big-time, outside financing being utilized by the young upstart who shared his last name was downright sinful.

That he made the telephone call to Anderson, instead of to Bob Johnson himself, was not surprising. Ever since Bob Johnson had started running around and proclaiming that BET would become the predominant brand for reaching the black consumer, John Johnson had taken offense. Johnson Publications, after all, had been king of black media for years. Until now, no one had ever had the gall to attempt to dethrone John Johnson. In fact, most newcomers into the black media arena had been obliged to go through him. For example, after Edward Lewis, Clarence

Smith, and other partners launched *Essence* in 1969, they kept it afloat by selling a stake to John Johnson. (Many years later, however, they also sold a stake in *Essence* to Time Warner, the company that succeeded Time Inc.)

Bob Johnson, however, by receiving his initial funding from a white firm, had changed the rules of the game. So from the outset, the relationship between the two men was strained. Only by coincidence, three of the largest black-owned companies ever created were built by people named Johnson: Johnson Publishing, BET, and Johnson Products, the hair care company that created Ultra Sheen and Afro Sheen and was founded by George Johnson. Because of their last names, many people got the three men confused or incorrectly assumed that they were related. But in the case of Bob Johnson and John Johnson, there was no love lost between them.

Shortly after he launched BET, Bob Johnson tried to get a meeting with John Johnson but was turned down. "He refused to see Bobby," recalls Virgil Hemphill, who was BET's first employee based in Chicago, home to Johnson Publishing. "John was very successful and way up there by then," and "he thought that Bobby was beneath him."

Years later, Bob Johnson did finally get in to see John Johnson and suggested that he might be interested in acquiring Johnson Publishing or merging the assets of the two companies some other way. The elder Johnson sat Bob Johnson down, and then proceeded to sternly lecture him. As John Johnson paced back and forth across the floor of his luxurious Michigan Avenue office, Bob Johnson listened politely. John told him that he would "never" sell his company. And then John went on to make it clear that he still ruled the roost. Bob Johnson returned to Washington, but not before letting it be known that if Johnson Publishing was ever for sale or interested in a partnership, he would be willing to talk.

The meeting, however, only heightened the tension between the two men. Several years later, according to the *Washington Post*, Bob Johnson addressed a group of Wall Street investors and told them that black-owned media companies would be forced to partner with majority-owned firms in order to survive. He then went on to specifically cite Johnson Publishing, and suggested that once the aging John Johnson was no longer alive, his company would probably die also. This time, John Johnson made his telephone call directly to Bob Johnson. "I called him up and cussed him out," John Johnson said. "I said, 'Really now, how dare you? You just got started, and I've been number one for 50 years. I am the biggest in my field. I don't want to be in the white field.' "[3]

Says Herb Wilkins, a venture capitalist who has partnered with both Johnsons in various business deals: "There's bad blood there."[4]

Despite the objections of John Johnson and others who shared his sentiments about BET's ownership structure, Robert Johnson thrived with the help of his deep-pocketed backers and turned his first profit just six years after BET's founding. In 1986, his company emerged from the red and generated a modest profit of less than $1 million. Johnson marked the occasion by giving each employee a reward—a dollar bill encased in Lucite. The inscription read: "Thank you for helping to make 1986 the first profitable year for Black Entertainment Television."

The following year, 1987, BET had total revenues of $10.7 million and net income of $956,000. However, the company was weighed down by the need to service more than $10 million in debt, mostly from the loans Johnson's partners had advanced. Only $2.5 million, or 25 percent of the company's total revenues, came from subscriber fees that year. These were the funds that BET collected from the cable operators that carried the channel. The remainder came from advertising sales.

In response, Anderson and his staff at HBO were trying to increase the total number of subscribers as well as the rate that

BET charged cable systems to carry the channel. But they were being met with resistance. Even though BET's rate of about 2 cents per subscriber paled in comparison to other cable channels that were charging as much as 15 to 20 cents, many cable operators felt that BET's programming was too narrow to justify paying much more. Moreover, they refused to acknowledge the value of the consumers who tuned in to BET.

It was not the heavy reliance on music programming that was causing consternation among the cable operators. Of greater concern at the time was the large amount of infomercials that were being used to pad BET's daily schedule. These 30- to 60-minute advertisements, which aired mostly late at night and in the wee hours of the morning, were accounting for 48 percent of BET's weekly programming. It was during these hours that BET looked nothing like a channel geared toward African-Americans. At these times it was just a cheap outlet for hawking the latest kitchen gadget or idea—from the ministries seeking to save souls and get viewers to mail in checks to the self-professed financial gurus promising to reveal—at a small cost, of course—the secrets to attaining wealth through real estate investments. Johnson needed to reduce the infomercials, but he first had to replace the revenue that they generated with additional income from subscriber fees and spot advertising.

Back inside BET, Johnson had replaced his sister Polly with a new vice president for finance, Antonia O. Duncan. A native of Panama, Duncan was known as a tough, no-nonsense taskmaster. But her sternness did not always sit well with BET's partners and cable affiliates. When Comcast Corporation and Cox Communications, two of the industry's largest system operators, were late paying their affiliate fees to BET, Duncan reacted by playing hardball and placing their accounts into collection. In an industry where everyone knew each other and such differences were always worked out on a personal basis, Duncan's action set off a small firestorm. Brian Roberts, head of Comcast, called Anderson at HBO. So did Jim Robbins, who headed Cox. "What the hell is going on?" he asked. Anderson called Johnson and had the two cable giants taken out of collection. But the incident did not sit well at HBO, which also was dependent on maintaining good relations with the cable operators.

In the ensuing days, a culture clash between HBO and BET began to take shape. Since the beginning of the partnership, some of the executives at HBO's parent, Time Inc., had been skeptical about investing in a small, unknown black company. They doubted Johnson's ability and the network's potential. Even some who fully supported the investment in BET never believed in it as a sound business. When Anderson was first trying to convince his managers at HBO to partner with BET, Tony Cox, who was a senior executive at the cable network, told Anderson, "I'll support you on this, but I don't think it will ever make money."

And Michael Fuchs, who was the head of HBO during the period of the partnership, recalls that BET was not much of a concern among the company's top executives. "No one was paying much attention," Fuchs admits. "There was a feeling that this channel was on automatic pilot. When you're a channel that's got a couple of big partners like us and Dr. Malone in there it's going to get distribution."[5]

Johnson sensed that his HBO partners did not fully respect him, and this, close associates say, only strengthened his resolve to succeed. The two companies continued to bump heads in their dealings with the cable system operators. At one point, BET undertook a campaign in which it contacted local black organizations such as churches, sororities, and fraternities. They pointed out the cable operators that did not carry the channel, urging the organizations to lobby the operators on BET's behalf. But in the view of Anderson and the folks at HBO, the campaign was a heavy-handed approach to dealing with the cable operators—not the way that HBO liked to handle relations with its affiliates. "It caused quite a storm," says Anderson. "The line between who was HBO and who was BET was getting blurred," and Time Inc. executives did not like it.

Finally, Anderson and Johnson agreed to meet in 1988 to discuss the future of their marketing and affiliate sales partnership. Anderson at the time was married to Barbara Smith, one of the first black supermodels and by then the owner of a popular Manhattan restaurant and bar, B. Smith's. Johnson and Anderson met at the restaurant, and as they sat in one of the booths, they agreed that it was time to end their marketing agreement and for BET to build its own affiliate sales department. "The time had come," Anderson says, "for BET to sever the cord and hire their own staff."

For the time being, HBO remained as an equity partner, but now Johnson was free to push as aggressively as he desired to convince cable affiliates to pay higher subscriber fees and to further build BET's subscriber base, which now totaled over 17 million.

Johnson's first move was to contact Curtis Symonds, a 31-year-old affiliate sales rep with the cable sports channel, ESPN. Symonds, an outgoing and personable man who loved to talk sports and wear high-fashioned tailored suits, had just been passed over for a promotion at ESPN. The job went to a white man who Symonds felt was no more qualified than he was, so when Johnson called, Symonds was primed to listen.

Johnson told Symonds that he needed him to join BET and to build an affiliate sales department. It would be a big promotion for Symonds, but he was cautious about leaving the stability of ESPN, which was easy to sell since every cable system operator had recognized that the fast-growing sports channel was a must-have. BET, on the other hand, was more of a risk. There was concern within the industry about the long-term financial stability of the black-owned network, and many cable operators still did not believe that they needed BET on their systems.

As he considered the job, Symonds asked Johnson, "What's your vision?" In response, Johnson began explaining how he envisioned BET expanding into magazines, movies, and other branded businesses. "I'm going to take this brand and expand it in every way," Johnson told Symonds. "This will be the preeminent brand for black people."

Symonds was sold. "Bob mapped out exactly how this thing would unfold," Symonds later said. "I could see that he was the consummate salesman, and a great visionary."

Over the next few years Symonds would not only vastly improve BET's financial standing, but he also became the personification of the network. He crisscrossed the country, calling on cable system operators and appearing at practically every cable industry event that took place. Born in Bermuda and raised in Ohio, Symonds had a fast-talking hustler's edge. In corporate settings, he could initially be a little misunderstood, but once people got to know him they found his charm infectious.

But even a charming salesman needed to have something to sell. So to help encourage cable operators to accept a rate increase, Johnson announced nine new BET-produced shows for the 1989 fall season. The cost of producing the new slate was $10 million. To help make the shows more cost-effective, Johnson also built his own production studio. He received local government tax incentives to develop the studio, which was also budgeted at $10 million, on a site located in a rundown area of northeast Washington. Even with the tax breaks, by the time the production facility opened in 1989 the price tag for building it had swelled to $12 million, adding a hefty amount of debt to the company's balance sheet.

One of the BET programs on the new slate was *Teen Summit*, a weekly hour-long public affairs show that used an *Oprah*-like talk show format to tackle serious issues such as sex, teen pregnancy, drugs, and AIDS.

Teen Summit was guaranteed long-term support and attention when it became a pet project for Sheila Johnson. Although she had been a listed in the corporate documents as a director of the company since its inception, she had remained mostly distanced from BET and focused on her own career. In addition to teaching music, she had written a textbook for string instruments, founded a 140-member children's orchestra, and traveled to Jordan, where she worked with Queen Noor to establish a music conservatory.

Sheila and Bob had been trying for some time to have children. Ultimately they turned to adoption. In 1985, an infant daughter, Paige, arrived. She was joined four years later by an infant brother, Brett. In 1990, just as *Teen Summit* was getting off the ground, Sheila joined BET as a full-time employee, taking on the title of vice president for corporate affairs. Her annual salary was $69,000.

Around the same time, Johnson entered into a partnership with the actor Tim Reid, who along with his wife, Daphne Maxwell Reid, had recently won critical acclaim for their CBS comedy, *Frank's Place.* The show won an Emmy award, but nevertheless failed to build an audience on the staid, so-called "Tiffany" network and was canceled. BET began airing *Frank's Place,* and Reid and Johnson agreed to a joint venture, with BET investing $1 million in an equal partnership aimed at developing comedies, dramas, and films.

With their new programming in the works, Symonds and Johnson together hit the road to convince their affiliates to accept a rate increase and to sell more system operators on the need to carry BET in their lineups. They found that in regions lacking large black populations, cable operators were concerned about offending white customers. One problem was that at this time the channel was still known by its full name, Black Entertainment Television. "A lot of people had a problem with the name," Symonds recalls. So, to overcome the perception that the network would appeal only to black people, the acronym BET was officially adopted in place of the full name.

By now, after years of hawking himself and his company, Johnson had become quite the seasoned executive. As they traveled around the country, Symonds realized that he was learning from one of the best salesmen and skilled communicators in the business.

Whenever they attended cable industry events, Johnson and Symonds were usually the only black people in the room. Yet Johnson was never intimidated. He moved with striking ease, holding his gin cocktail and comfortably and eloquently engaging people on just about any topic. Few people could enter the same room as Johnson without him making sure that he met them. Johnson's style was personable and self-effacing, and when he talked to people they felt comfortable as he put them at ease by referring to himself as "a country boy." And he had plenty of down-home charm to back it up. He was good at remembering people's names, and he'd ask them about their families.

"He reached out to everybody," says Herb Wilkins. "He's that kind of person. He does not let anybody get by. I mean he knows people not just in a casual way. He knows them and what their business is. He knows their family. And he wants to know." Or, as Symonds recalls, "He'd make people feel like 'God, this guy cares.'"

Johnson could seem so easygoing that it caused many of his business associates to underestimate the smart, shrewd predator that lurked behind the smile. He'd sometimes joke with close associates about how he liked to play the dumb hick because it caused people to drop their guard and reveal valuable knowledge and information. And when it was time to negotiate, Johnson always knew every deal point as well as if not better than everyone else around the table. He always knew what he would have to do to win a deal, and he would almost always let the other side take the first volley. So while the other guy was supposedly showing his smarts by putting his offer on the table first, Johnson was not revealing his true position. That way, the people across the table never knew what they had to do to get to a winning position. Johnson's approach took that away from them.

Single-minded in his approach, Johnson always knew from the outset what he wanted to achieve in a negotiation. He would meet to discuss the terms of a contract, and when the meeting started he would not have a single sheet of paper in front of him. But what people across the negotiating table did not know was that Johnson had already read every word of the necessary information and stored it away in his near-photographic memory. Once, while sitting in a meeting with Herb Wilkins and other business associates, Johnson stunned the room when a specific issue pertaining to an obscure contract clause came up for discussion. "Bob recounted, verbatim, a paragraph out of the documents, and it just floored me," recalls Wilkins. "I mean, I could not believe that he could recall this obscure paragraph in the documents. But he did; he knew every word." It's that way with every contract, Wilkins says. "Bob has read it all and can recite the words. He's that smart. He plays that 'I'm a local farm boy' thing. But he is as smart as they come."

Johnson also had an uncanny ability to remain unflappable, no matter the circumstances. He was even-tempered and slow to anger, and rarely used profanity. Even when people at the negotiating table offended him or did things that would anger most others, Johnson would not get upset.

Shortly after forming their partnership, Johnson and Reid scheduled a meeting with executives from New Line Cinema to discuss the possibility of making a film in conjunction with the Hollywood studio. As they gathered inside the office of Robert Shaye, New Line's chief, a young white woman who worked at the studio joined them. A patronizing know-it-all, the woman told the group that she doubted that Johnson and Reid could make successful independent black films. "What makes you think that black actors will come work for you?" she asked, as Johnson and Reid sat there amazed by her gall. "You guys don't really have respect in the black community."

Reid became visibly angry. "I wanted to grab her by the throat, look her in the face and say 'I will smack the shit out of you,' " Reid said, recalling the incident. "I wanted to let her see what a real nigger was." Johnson, however, never flinched or wavered.[6]

When they left the office and got on the elevator, Reid was still fuming. He looked over at Johnson, who appeared tranquil, as if nothing had occurred. "Didn't that make you angry?" Reid burst out. "Tim," Johnson replied calmly, "why are you getting so excited about that? She has no power over you. What she thinks of me has no effect on me. I will still do what I want to do."

On another occasion in New York, Johnson was arriving at the offices of the Arts & Entertainment Network, a joint venture of the Hearst Corporation, ABC, and NBC, to discuss a possible film partnership. Dressed in a suit and tie, he arrived at the front desk in the lobby and informed the guard, who was white, that he was there to see the president of the channel. "Go around to the side of the building," the guard told him. "Huh?" Johnson asked. "Go around the side," the guard repeated. "That way," he pointed. "Go ahead. That's where the elevator is."[7] Johnson walked around the building, and there he found the freight elevator. The guard apparently thought he was making a delivery. Johnson climbed on board the elevator, and standing amid a load of furniture and boxes, he headed for his meeting.

Showing emotion, in Johnson's view, was a sign of weakness that let people know that they could get to him. "He just never let anything shake him," says Reid. In fact, Johnson had a coldness about him. He always showed people respect and was never the type to gratuitously attack people, but over the years he demonstrated a willingness to take out anyone he perceived as an adversary or an obstacle to his own success.

Even his own wife, Sheila, confided: "He has no emotion. He has a very hard heart."

One racial incident, however, did push Johnson to his breaking point. In December 1988 when he was in New York for a meeting at HBO, the BET chief checked into the Grand Hyatt in midtown Manhattan. After unpacking his clothes, he headed downstairs. While walking through the hotel's expansive lobby, Johnson was stopped by four hotel employees who took him into custody for questioning. After two police officers arrived Johnson was told that he could leave. Johnson demanded to know why he had been detained. The reason, he was told, was that a black man had committed a crime in the hotel. This was one racial slight that Johnson did not simply shrug off. Instead, he sued the Hyatt Corporation and Regency Lexington Partners, the operators of the hotel, for a reported $2 million, for false arrest and violating his civil rights. Several months later, the suit was dropped but neither side would say if there was a monetary settlement.

Often, Johnson and Symonds took Jeff Lee, the head of programming, along on their journeys. This way, the cable operators could hear the plans for improving the network's programming firsthand from the chief of programming himself. They worked to convince cable system operators to accept a rate increase and begin paying the channel five cents per subscriber, with an additional one-cent annual increase over a four-year period ending in 1994. The cable affiliates eventually signed on, but only after some tough talks and demands that the programming would get significantly better and that BET would cut back on the seemingly incessant infomercials. Whenever Lee and Symonds worried about meeting the demands of their customers, Johnson pushed them to make the sale. Just tell the customers what they want to hear, he implored. "Promise them the world," Johnson ordered his two executives.

As they moved around the country, it was becoming apparent that the BET brand was gaining cachet in the black community. Everywhere the BET executives went, they noticed that people not only recognized the company but also displayed tremendous gratitude for and pride in BET. "Everybody you met, wherever you went, when you said you worked for BET they lit up like a Christmas tree," says Lee. When the BET executives checked into hotels, if the desk clerk was black, they often got an upgrade. Black people wanted to support them in whatever small way they could. It became apparent that the audience was not only growing, but was also beginning to regard BET in a proprietary way. "The outside world saw us as holding an heirloom for them," Lee says. "Black people took ownership in BET."

Some in the black community were skeptical, finding it difficult to believe that their own people were finally, actually in control of a nationwide media outlet. They had heard or read about Malone and other investors, and did not hesitate to query the BET executives on the topic. "A white man really owns this company, doesn't he?" Lee recalls one observer asking him. "Aren't you all just fronting for the white man?"

The three executives grew close as they traveled together. In the evenings they'd huddle at a restaurant or in a hotel bar and brainstorm, devising plans to grow the business. "We came up with many ideas over drinks or having dinner in Los Angeles or some other city," says Symonds. "We'd get back in D.C. and say 'Okay, let's make this happen.'"

Back in Washington, where more than 100 people were now working for the company, the core team of executives that would oversee BET's biggest period of growth during the 1990s was firmly in place. In addition to Symonds and Lee, it included James A. Ebron, the head of advertising sales. A New York City native, Ebron had been mentored early in his career by John Johnson, who had hired him as an advertising salesman for *Ebony* and *Jet*. The BET team was rounded off by Janis Thomas, who worked closely with Ebron servicing the advertising accounts.

Johnson was also beginning to seek more and more guidance from Debra L. Lee, his general counsel. Lee, who joined the company in 1986, received her undergraduate degree from Brown University, and went on to earn a master's and a law degree from Harvard. She had previously worked for Steptoe & Johnson, the Washington firm that handled much of BET's legal work in the early years. Young, confident, and pretty, Lee was not a likely candidate to gain Johnson's good graces. Before her arrival, he really did not like lawyers, his associates recall, because they were always telling him why something would not work. "Don't worry about legal. We'll deal with them later," Johnson would say. "They don't control the business."

But Lee showed an unswerving loyalty to her boss, always supporting Johnson's decisions and making it clear to employees that she was carrying out his wishes. As Lee gained Johnson's ear and won his confidence, other female employees at the company took pride in her accomplishments and began to look to her for guidance.

In all, the team that Johnson had put together was jelling. More importantly, they were succeeding. As more urban markets got wired for cable, and system operators increasingly added the channel to their lineups, the company began a period of explosive growth. By 1991, BET reached 31.6 million subscribers, or 53 percent of all U.S. homes that received cable at that time. The company had operating revenues of $50 million, compared to just $10 million five years earlier. BET's net income, or actual profit, was now $9.3 million.

The days that Johnson, Symonds, and Lee spent on the road cajoling cable system operators to fork over higher fees were paying off. Some 40 percent of BET's total revenues now came from subscriber fees. Five years earlier, subscriber fees had accounted for just 25 percent of total revenues. Revenues from subscriber fees rose over the five-year period at a compound annual growth rate of 69 percent to a total of $20 million.

At the same time, the nearly $30 million that the company earned in advertising revenues in 1991 represented a compound annual growth rate of 38 percent over the five-year period. Even the cable affiliates were pleased that the reliance on infomercials was also easing. In 1987, an average of 48 percent of the network's weekly programming was filled with the annoying, yet effective 30- to 60-minute advertisements. But by 1991, infomercials accounted for just 35 percent of the weekly programming.

After 11 years of business, Bob Johnson had created real value. Now, however, he needed to find a way to accelerate the company's growth. He consulted with Malone, a genius at financing and timing the public financial markets. Around this time, the country was emerging from a recession and the stock market was warming up, priming itself for the boom in prices and the tide of initial public offerings (IPOs) that would occur over the next decade. "It's time to look to the equity markets," Malone told him. All of Johnson's partners agreed—BET was ready to sell its stock to the public.

An initial public offering was something that only a couple of black-owned companies had ever done, and no black company had ever been listed on the prestigious New York Stock Exchange. If BET could do it, this would provide the company with money to fund additional growth and make Johnson himself incredibly rich. An IPO would validate the founder's dream. BET would be more than a little operation that was of interest only to black people. With Wall Street traders buying and selling shares of BET, it would be a big-time, all-American business.

THE FAMILY

W ilmer Ames Jr. was not the average magazine entrepreneur. He was black. He was gay. And he was a Republican. But Ames, who by age 40 had spent about a decade as a researcher and reporter at *Sports Illustrated*, had an idea for a magazine geared toward black readers.

With a small selection of titles—such as *Essence, Ebony*, and *Black Enterprise*—for black readers to choose from, many editorial and publishing professionals like Ames were convinced that the market was underserved. Ames' magazine, he proposed, would provide for an upscale black readership what magazines like *Time* and *Newsweek* provided to the mainstream—thoughtful and analytical insight into news events. Ames dubbed his would-be monthly magazine *Emerge*, and he accompanied it with a fitting slogan: "Black America's Newsmagazine."

It was 1989 when Ames took the idea to his bosses at Time Inc., a virtual magazine factory that at the time was publishing 17 titles, including everything from *People* magazine to *Cooking Light*. Ames needed about $5 million to launch *Emerge*. Chris Meigher, who was group publisher of several magazines at the time, heard the idea and liked it. Meigher happened to have a close relationship with Joe Collins, who was heading Time's HBO unit. When Meigher told Collins about Ames' idea, Collins suggested that Meigher contact another HBO executive, Don Anderson, who had been in charge of HBO's partnership with BET. After Meigher, Collins, Anderson, and Ames met in New York to talk about the proposed magazine, they agreed that to make it work and have true credibility in the black community, it needed black ownership. Anderson contacted Bob Johnson and arranged for a meeting.

Johnson was anxious to find a way to begin expanding his BET brand across other platforms. The magazine business offered a good way to cross-market products, thus adding to advertising revenues and increasing household penetration for the network. So when Ames and Anderson arrived in Washington, Johnson had informed his friend and partner, the venture capitalist Herb Wilkins, of the proposed magazine and Ames' search for black financial partners. Another business partner and friend of Johnson's, Tyrone Brown, a former Federal Communications Commissioner and a Washington lawyer who had provided legal counsel to BET over the years, was also invited to consider partnering with Ames in the magazine.

Ames presented his concept, and Anderson let the group know that Time Inc. was willing to take 20 percent of the equity and provide printing and distribution. Johnson agreed to purchase 27 percent of the equity. Wilkins, Brown, and Ames took the remainder of the equity. A magazine was born, and BET made its first big step toward extending its brand beyond the cable network.

Eventually, as *Emerge* reached a circulation of about 150,000, Johnson bought out Time Warner, Wilkins, and Brown, taking control of *Emerge*. He became publisher and moved Ames out of the editor's office, replacing him with George Curry, a former *Chicago Tribune* correspondent. On the day that Curry took over, February 16, 1993, Ames died after a lengthy illness. Johnson solidified his control of the magazine, negotiating to purchase the remaining equity from Ames' estate.

"Bob wanted to make it a more forceful magazine," Curry says. "So I was in a good position."

Johnson moved to expand his interest in the magazine business, launching a title geared toward black teenagers and young adults. *YSB*, as it was called, stood for "young sisters and brothers." It debuted in August 1991. It was a small business compared to the network, but Johnson saw it as a pet project, a way to nurture young BET customers and to also produce wholesome, uplifting content. He named the venture Paige Publishing, after the baby daughter that he and Sheila had adopted a few years earlier. Further signifying its importance to him, he put Debra Lee, the general counsel who was increasingly gaining his trust, in charge of *YSB*. It was her first time managing a profit-oriented operation at BET. The magazine received critical praise for its dedication to building self-esteem in black teenagers, and the circulation quickly climbed to over 100,000.

As it was expanding and growing into the hottest and most exciting black-owned and -operated business in the country, BET was now becoming *the* place to be. Entertainers who once had to be persuaded to make appearances were now requesting the opportunity to be on the network. New college graduates, who in previous years would have automatically sought their first jobs amid the cushy security of corporate giants like Xerox or Gannett, were instead seeking employment opportunities at BET. Others even left the confines of larger corporations for BET.

The pay was not always great. But the opportunity to work at a fast-growing, entrepreneurial, and black-owned company was priceless. Curtis Gadson, who left Post-Newsweek Stations and joined BET in 1992 as supervising producer, recalls the first day that he walked into BET's production facility. "I saw a sea of black people doing the same jobs that I had always seen only whites doing elsewhere," Gadson says. "I was almost in tears. The playing field was suddenly level."[1]

Johnson's determination to run BET like a major corporation

was felt throughout the organization and sometimes bordered on the obsessive. He prohibited employees from popping microwave popcorn inside the Georgetown executive offices because the odor would waft through the atrium and make the place seem, and smell, unprofessional. When a female executive, Gloria Nauden, showed up at work with her hair changed from its natural black color to a stunning bright blonde, Johnson let her know that he did not like the change. He told Debra Lee, his general counsel and trusted confidant, to tell Nauden that the blonde locks were not proper around the office and that she should dye her hair back to black. A few days later Nauden complied. "I just kind of took the instruction in the spirit that it was given to me," Nauden concedes.

To be sure, some of the stereotypical practices attributed to small black businesses did exist. The company gained a reputation for being slow paying vendors and outside contractors. And Johnson, for many years, insisted on personally signing every single check—hundreds of them each month—instead of using a stamped signature as the heads of most large corporations do. But mostly, Johnson wanted BET to emulate corporate America, and many young professionals learned what they could at the company and then left to parlay their experience into higher-paying jobs at bigger media outlets and elsewhere in corporate America.

On the production side, a number of people who would go on to notable broadcasting and entertainment careers were at this time getting their early experience at BET. James Brown, the famous broadcaster who became an anchor on *The NFL Today* on Fox, was first a sports anchor at BET. The show *Teen Summit* provided the first job in television for its host Ananda Lewis. She went on to become a celebrity on MTV and to have her own short-lived syndicated television talk show. The comedian Cedric "The Entertainer" Kyles first gained national prominence as the host of BET's *ComicView* show. There were many others.

There was so much cross-utilization of talent that it was like being part of a farm club. The experience of Madelyne Woods, who joined the network in 1990 shortly after finishing graduate school at Howard University, illustrates the jack-of-all-trades quality of a BET job. Woods started in the news department as a reporter, but just two weeks later she began anchoring one-minute newsbreaks. Over the next four years, her responsibilities expanded to include sports reporting and hosting music video shows. "I got all kinds of experience," Woods says. "I also got my first taste of office politics."

The internal politics were like those that exist inside huge, competitive families. Employees competed for every crumb, and in the process developed close relationships. Everyone knew each other, and everyone knew each other's personal business. There was a lot of camaraderie, but also plenty of rivalry. Staffers jockeyed for opportunities and recognition from their immediate supervisors or from Johnson himself. After work, they spent their leisure time unwinding together at each other's homes.

And there was relentless pressure to look good and dress well. From the production studio to the executive offices, all the women were beauties who sported the finest hairstyles, while the men were well-groomed and handsome. The staff was like a camera-ready, walking advertisement for the company. "Everybody at BET was pretty," recalls Woods. "When you walked in you noticed that everybody was gorgeous. Not just the on-air talent, but also the makeup artists, the camera operators, the TelePrompTer operator—everybody. It made you start dressing a little better and tending to your makeup."[2]

And like a family, they pulled together in times of need. Woods was on her way to a BET event in 1990 when she stopped at a local mall to pick up a pair of panty hose. Getting back into her car, she was attacked by a carjacker who beat her so severely

that her teeth were impacted into her gums. She was hospital-
ized and off the air for six weeks, and for a long time afterward
was required to wear an appliance to keep her teeth stable.
While she was out, she received a video from BET. "Everybody in
the building appeared on that tape, wishing me well. They were
talking about what they would do to the guy who beat me,"
Woods says. "We were close. It was a family." On her first day
back in the studio, Johnson sent Woods a bouquet of roses, with
a note: "Glad you're back on the air."

Further fostering the feeling of family, the company had an
annual picnic for the entire staff and their families. Organized by
Curtis Symonds, the outing grew each year and became a major
event, with the employees from the Los Angeles and New York
offices even sometimes coming into Washington to attend. The
day would start with a round of golf; then, as more people arrived, bushels of crabs were delivered. The BET mobile truck,
equipped with a sound system and disc jockey equipment, was
set up, and the staff would party at a northern Virginia park until
late in the evening. Johnson would always attend. He did not
play golf but would join in volleyball or softball games, and he
would sit and chat with employees until the event ended. He
knew their spouses and children by name. For the rank and file, it
was treasured time spent mingling with the boss.

In similar fashion, the entire staff came together at annual
Christmas parties. Here, Johnson would usually not only chat
with workers but also give a short talk discussing the state of
the company. He liked these events to feel very corporate and
sophisticated, but sometimes they evolved into plain old, serious throw-down jams. At the 1989 Christmas party, which was
held at a Washington hotel and coincided with the company's
10th anniversary, one of the country's hottest singers at the
time, Gerald Levert, performed. His father, Eddie Levert of the
famed O'Jays, also made a surprise appearance and the two
sang a duet. It was a black-tie event, but when Gerald Levert

performed his single, "Casanova," which had been a chart top-per for many months, everyone from the top executives to the mailroom workers loosened their ties and hit the dance floor to do the popular dance at the time, the cabbage patch. Not the type to do much dancing, the always-reserved Johnson sat back and, like a proud father, watched with satisfied amusement.

As long as employees were loyal and respectful, they bene-fited from Johnson's paternalism. He set up a loan program, pro-viding workers with interest-free loans for their personal needs. They would submit written requests and then sit down with Johnson to explain their financial needs. Once a loan was granted, Johnson would simply deduct payments from the em-ployee's paychecks. It was a generous personal touch that would later disappear as the company grew larger.

The feeling of being one happy family was especially strong among the top executives. Johnson and his executives still worked long, hard days. But now the company was doing well enough that they were also able to relax and enjoy a taste of the good life. Together, they would often retire to a nearby Georgetown seafood restaurant, the Sea Catch, for drinks and dinner. And on special occasions, they would gather for dinner at the Four Seasons, where Johnson would treat himself and others to lobster.

During the steamy Washington summers, Johnson and his executive vice presidents would often jump in their cars and head two hours northeast to Rehoboth Beach in Delaware. There, they'd gather for drinks, seafood, and barbecue at a mod-est beach house that Johnson had purchased through BET. These were special getaways, as they would use the time to discuss the future of the company and to draw closer together personally. They enjoyed it so much, in fact, that when Bob and Sheila Johnson purchased a larger beach home nearby, he arranged to have his executive vice presidents chip in and purchase the orig-inal home. They obliged, and in true team spirit, they set up schedules for use of the house. Whichever vice president was on the schedule to have the house for the weekend was likely to take his or her family and get together with the Johnson family while at the beach.

The shared beach house was not the only property that Johnson passed on to underlings. When he and Sheila decided to sell their home in the Forest Hills section of Washington and build a larger, more lavish residence—complete with a tennis court and swimming pool—just around the corner in the same neighborhood, they did not put their place on the market. Instead, they kept it in the family, so to speak, and sold it to Debra Lee and her husband, Randall Coleman, a Washington attorney. As a result, Lee, Coleman, and their two young children became even closer to the Johnsons. By creating such opportunities for his executives, Johnson ingrained his image as the patriarch, and in return his employees grew increasingly loyal.

He enjoyed socializing, but around the office Johnson was always reserved. He dressed conservatively, favoring subdued blue and gray suits. He would not wear full-cut European suit jackets without vents in the back. He shunned double-breasted and three-button jackets, and his neckties were usually tied in big, wide knots. It was the type of attire that dominated the wardrobes of Washington's political establishment. However, Johnson was no longer in politics; he was in the entertainment business. At home, Sheila would gently try to push him to be more fashionable. And at the office, Symonds, whose flashy wardrobe was sometimes even more than the entertainment industry could handle, would constantly ride Johnson about his clothing. "Bob used to wear some crazy shit and I used to tell him," Symonds says. "He was very, very conservative."

The proper decorum was always paramount to Johnson. But still, he could sometimes come off as "a regular brother." One employee recalls once during the early 1990s when Sheila Johnson had just given her husband a convertible Chrysler LeBaron for his birthday. He came driving up to the office with the top down and grooving as the Mtume song "Juicy Fruit" blasted on his radio. And another employee, a former audio engineer in production, says he was stunned one day when he saw Johnson and Butch Lewis, the professional boxing promoter who became one of Johnson's business partners and closest friends, standing off to the side at the studio "laughing and talking like two brothers on the corner." As the former employee recalls, "they were grabbing their crotches and saying 'm-f' this and 'm-f' that."

But those moments were exceptions; Johnson was typically reserved and in control. In fact, his behavior was in stark contrast to some of the people with whom he surrounded himself. Symonds, with his outgoing personality, was always demonstrative and loud. As *Emerge* editor Curry recalled, "If Curtis was around, you'd hear him. And I don't care what part of the building you were in." And Jeff Lee, although slightly more subdued, was also animated at times—especially when he and Symonds paired up. "When Curtis and Jeff got together, it was a performance. They'd come in talking loud and high-fiving each other," says Curry. They may have been two of the top bosses, but still it was apparent to everyone that "they were two fun-loving guys."

Symonds was the public representative for the company, attending cable industry dinners and serving on nonprofit industry boards. He also became known inside the company as the executive who mixed most easily with the workers. In addition to organizing the Christmas party and annual picnic, he also convinced Johnson to sponsor company basketball and softball teams. Among the rank and file, he was popular and well liked. Yet Symonds was also one of the few people—other than Johnson's sister and former employee, Paulette Johnson—who could stir anger and emotion in the usually placid Johnson. On one occasion, Johnson and Symonds held such a loud shouting match inside Johnson's office that everyone outside within earshot thought for sure that Symonds would be fired when it was over. Minutes later they were talking and joking as if nothing had ever happened.

Among the seven vice presidents who served under Johnson, Jeff Lee emerged as the heir apparent to the chief executive. The company did not have a number-two executive, but as the head of network operations, Lee was responsible for running the network and was very close to Johnson. Everyone was sure that it was just a matter of time before Johnson would make Lee his official second-in-command. Lee even began to tone down his own style, mimicking Johnson's low-key approach and spending less time mingling with the workers around the studio. As one colleague says: "Jeff became a mini-Bob."

But while Jeff Lee, James Ebron, and Curtis Symonds were running huge and vital segments of the business, Debra Lee, the general counsel, was not faring too well in her first operational role as publisher of the teen magazine *YSB*. After losing about $2 million per year, Johnson shut *YSB* down after five years. But despite the magazine's failure, Debra Lee continued to gain Johnson's trust, providing legal counsel on all aspects of the business. She was great at multitasking. At the time she was carrying her first child, she was also overseeing the construction of a new headquarters building for BET, running the publishing division, and continuing to function as the company's general counsel. Her Ivy League style was markedly different from that of the others. She was quiet and discreet, always there to support Johnson. As Johnson did more and more deals, Lee became increasingly important to her boss.

In all, life at BET was good. But Johnson's employees would soon learn that there was a limit to his paternalistic ways. Any attempt to assert themselves independently was perceived by

Johnson as disloyalty. And he would not hesitate to remind them of who was in charge. In 1993, when production employees tried unsuccessfully to form a union at BET, one of them wrote an anonymous letter to one of the record labels that supplied music videos to BET. The letter, a typical union-organizing ploy, was critical of how BET treated its employees.

When Johnson learned of the letter, he was livid. He called all of the company's production employees together for an emergency meeting inside the new production facility. Many of the workers saw a different side of their boss for the first time. He was clearly angry. "If you don't like the way things are being run here, then go start your own BET," Johnson said to his employees. "When you become a millionaire, I'll be the first one to welcome you to the club." Then, he went on to make it perfectly clear to the employees that they were working at his pleasure. "I started BET for myself and for my family," Johnson said, as workers listened in shock.[3]

And then one night even those closest to Johnson, his senior executives, were left aghast by Johnson's insistence on always being number one in their minds. It was nearly 3 A.M. when the telephones starting ringing inside the homes of BET's senior vice presidents. "Please hold for a conference call with Mr. Johnson," the voice on the other end said. When Johnson got on the phone, he was irate. Earlier that evening, the executives had attended a Janet Jackson concert at the USAir Arena in Largo, Maryland. BET was able to purchase the tickets to the sold-out concert through one of the record labels that BET did business with. A few of the tickets were given to Sheila Johnson, and along with friends she also attended the concert. However, some of the BET employees were sitting closer to the stage than Sheila and her group were sitting.

"I'm disturbed that Sheila did not have the best seats," Johnson told his still half-asleep executives during the conference call. "When the company purchases tickets she should have the best seats in the house," he said. They all agreed and explained that it had been an oversight. But they could not believe that Johnson could not wait until the next business day to make his point. "I was lying in bed thinking, 'This is not real. I am dreaming,'" says Curtis Symonds. "We could not believe that he called at three in the morning to tell us some shit like that."[4]

But the message was clear, even to his groggy managers: At BET, Bob Johnson was king. And woe to those who would dare to forget it.

"BET IN THE HOUSE"

By late 1991, as Bob Johnson prepared to offer stock in BET to the public and make his firm the first-ever black-owned company traded on the New York Stock Exchange, nearly 32 million homes were receiving the network. Black Entertainment Television had truly arrived. Finally, black Americans had a channel specifically for them. No longer would they have to sit and watch television without seeing a character who looked like them. The *Cosby Show*, which debuted on NBC in 1984, was a watershed in terms of the portrayal of blacks on television. But there was no television network where such positive programming could be found each day. Many people assumed that BET would become that place. No longer would blacks on television be stereotypical buffoons, hustlers, or sidekicks to leading white actors. No longer would the experiences of black people be filtered through a white lens. BET was now officially a formidable business, and it was owned and run by black people. There was a quiet rejoicing in black America. Television, the most powerful image builder ever created, now held a real opportunity to uplift the tattered image of America's black people. Bob Johnson had given people more than a cable channel. He had given them a source of pride and hope, and the feeling that something important belonged to them.

That pride, hope, and sense of ownership were all on display in New York City on the morning of November 1, 1991. Bob Johnson and a gaggle of BET executives and Wall Street bankers were on the floor of the New York Stock Exchange, excitedly awaiting the 9:30 A.M. opening bell to begin trading. It was a major day for BET Holdings Incorporated, the new name that Johnson had given his company to prepare it to go public. And now, in just a few minutes, the company's stock would begin trading for the first time.

Two of Johnson's top lieutenants, Curtis Symonds and Jefferi Lee, had been forced to stay behind in Washington to tend to personal business the previous day. Determined not to miss the momentous occasion, however, they had jumped on a shuttle flight early that next morning, arrived at LaGuardia Airport, and taken a taxi into Lower Manhattan. As the taxi arrived in the Wall Street financial district, the traffic slowed to a crawl. Finally, with the car at a standstill and the opening bell for trading only a few minutes away, Lee asked the driver to point them in the right direction, and he and Symonds jumped out of the vehicle and began sprinting toward the stock exchange.

After a few blocks, they arrived—huffing and puffing—but not knowing where to go they mistakenly went to an employee entrance, where only those with the proper identification were allowed. A security guard who was checking employee badges told Lee and Symonds that they would have to go around the building to the main entrance. But just as they were about to leave, another guard, a young black man, stopped them. "Y'all with BET?" he asked. "Yes," Lee and Symonds said simultaneously, their anxious voices underscoring the fact that they were running late.

The black security guard's eyes lit up with excitement. He started yelling, "Come on in! Come on in!" The guard shouted, "Spread out and let them through!" as he directed the BET executives past the exchange employees who were milling in to work. "This is the big day," he said. "BET in the house."[1]

The guard, like so many BET viewers, felt a close connection to the network. Because it was black owned and operated, they supported it and regarded it as if it were their own. When people talked about BET, recalls Jeff Lee, they called it "our BET." But now, with the company offering a 21 percent stake or 4.2 million shares to the public, some of these viewers and fans of the network could actually own a piece of the company.

Although large institutional investors bought up most of the shares, Johnson made sure that about 400,000 shares were sold to individuals. And of those shares, about 277,000 were purchased by black investors.[2] The lead underwriters for the stock offering were Wall Street heavyweights, the First Boston Corporation and Bear, Stearns & Company. Lem Daniels, a Bear, Stearns broker based in Los Angeles, sold much of the stock to the black celebrities and entertainers who comprise much of his client base.

Although he used major banks to do the deal, Johnson also wanted to assure that some of Wall Street's smaller, black-owned firms took part in underwriting the shares. "Bob was very vocal about wanting to see minority firms have real participation in the deal as opposed to just serving as window dressing," recalls Albert Sturdivant, a black banker whose firm, Sturdivant & Company Inc., underwrote 50,000 shares of the BET offering. "We sat down and talked with Bob about the deal. He wanted firms like ours involved in the transaction." In the end, a total of about 10 minority-owned brokerage firms participated in the stock sale.

Johnson was proud that black investors bought BET stock. He told Leon Wynter of the *Wall Street Journal* that the participation in BET's initial public offering (IPO) by black people "creates a fertile environment for more black firms to go public." With blacks owning a stake in BET, Johnson said, "it becomes like family."[3]

To sell the deal to Wall Street, Johnson played the "black-owned" theme to the hilt. He told investors that the company's ongoing success was dependent on it remaining in the hands of black people. "Management believes that black ownership and control of the company has been an essential element in its growth and success," BET stated in the prospectus that it filed with the Securities and Exchange Commission.

Citing that need to maintain black ownership and control, Johnson mimicked what other media companies were doing at the time and cleverly divided his stock into three classes. Each share of class A stock was entitled to one vote. These were the shares that were being offered to the public. Each share of class B and class C stock would be entitled to 10 votes. Johnson's partners, John Malone and HBO, would hold all of the class B stock, and Johnson would hold all of the class C stock. So the two classes of shares with super-voting rights would continue to be closely held by Johnson and his partners. The holders of the publicly traded class A shares would have the right to elect just two members to the board. However, Johnson and his partners would control the board, electing five of its members.

What this all meant was that Johnson was able to have his cake and eat it, too. Although he was selling the 21 percent stake in the company to the public and instantly pocketing millions for himself, he would still maintain full control of the company with 56 percent of the combined voting power—even though he would hold less than 50 percent of the total equity following the offering. The public would now own BET, but Bob Johnson would remain firmly in control.

When Johnson and his bankers went on the road to sell the deal, potential investors liked what they heard. Over the prior five years, BET's revenues had grown at a compound annual rate of 47 percent. Over the same period, its operating income (income before depreciation and amortization—a commonly used measure of performance in the industry) had grown at a rate of 88 percent, and its net income had grown at a rate of 77 percent.

The network's ratings weren't great, but they were adequate. Nielsen Media Research, the company that provides metered audience measures, estimated that BET's average rating was a 0.5. This meant that of the 31.6 million cable homes receiving BET, one-half of 1 percent, or about 158,000, actually watched the network during the evening prime time hours. By comparison, other basic cable channels at the time averaged ratings in the range of 0.3 to 1.3.

Still, other than MTV, which was only dabbling in black music, there was little competition to worry about. Plus, there was plenty of room for growth. An additional 30 million homes were already wired with cable but not yet receiving BET, and millions of miles of new cable were still being laid across the country. And BET's core audience, the black population, was burgeoning—increasing in numbers, watching more television than white Americans, proving to be very brand loyal, and gaining affluence and spending power.

So by the time the IPO day arrived, it was clear that it would be a big success. A total of 4.2 million shares had been presold in the offering, for $17 each. For its own corporate coffers, BET, after paying fees to the bankers, netted $33.6 million for the 2.1 million shares that it sold. The company used about $7 million to pay down one-third of its outstanding debt. The remainder of the money was put away to fund acquisitions and other brand-building ventures.

At the opening bell, BET stock, traded under the symbol BTV, shot from $17 up to $25. Johnson and the others were ecstatic. Finally, the stock cooled off just a bit, and closed at $23.50, up 38 percent in one day. At the end of its first trading day, BET had a market value of $472 million. The company's top executive officers received stock options at an exercise price equal to the public offering price, so they went home happy.

No one was as happy as Johnson, who himself sold 375,000

shares (4 percent of his own shares) to the public. He received $6 million, and used $2.5 million of the money to repay a loan that the company had extended to him a few months earlier. In addition to his ownership stake, he was paying himself $535,000 in annual salary and bonus. Additionally, Sheila Johnson was earning $70,000 as a vice president of the company. But Johnson's equity was where the real wealth would be found. Sheila Johnson had "beneficial ownership" in the shares that her husband held; however, he maintained full control over the shares. Before the stock started trading on the first day, the 9.3 million shares that he was keeping were worth $149 million. And by the end of the first trading day, Johnson's personal stake was valued at $218 million. Bob and Sheila Johnson were now, officially, filthy rich. Asked how it felt, Johnson laughed with delight and borrowed a quote from the legendary entertainer Pearl Bailey: "I've been rich and I've been poor," Johnson said. "And rich is better."[4]

The IPO also allowed one of Johnson's first investors to exit the partnership with a very handsome profit. Cincinnati financier Carl Lindner's Great American Broadcasting, formerly Taft Broadcasting, one of BET's original investors, sold its entire 22 percent of BET's class A common stock, or 2.4 million shares, in the offering. For its original $1 million investment made just nine years earlier, Great American netted a total of $38.5 million. It was a happy ending to its relationship with Johnson, and the proceeds of the sale helped Great American, which was saddled with huge interest payments on leverage buyout debt it had accumulated. For betting on his dream, Johnson had repaid his partners very well.

BET's other two original partners, the HBO unit of Time Warner and Malone, did not sell any of their equity in the offering. With their super-voting shares, HBO kept 15 percent of the total equity yet 18 percent of the voting control, and Malone kept 18 percent of the equity and 21 percent of the votes. The

21 percent of the equity sold to the public carried just 4.5 percent of the voting control in the company.

Now Johnson had the best of both worlds—enormous personal wealth and the ongoing control over his company. By all early indications, taking his company public had been a brilliant move. The stock was roaring. He had millions in his bank account and plenty of cash to expand the BET brand. It was an intoxicating time. The euphoria, however, did not last long.

Just six weeks after the initial offering, on Friday, December 16, 1991, BET received a harsh welcome into the world of publicly traded companies. BET released it first quarterly report to investors. It was for the fiscal first quarter, which had ended on October 31 of that year.

There was no problem with the earnings themselves. Net income had increased 13 percent to $2.3 million. If not for the half million that had been lost trying to get the magazine *YSB* going, the company would have had a 37 percent increase in net income. But investors grew concerned when they realized that BET's subscriber revenues were lower than research analysts had been estimating, and the discrepancy alarmed them so much that they began dumping BET shares.

By Monday morning, BET stock had plunged 50 percent. Something had to be done to calm the market, and fast. First, Johnson asked the New York Stock Exchange to halt trading in BET shares. Then he announced an emergency conference call for investors and analysts.

Johnson and his chief financial officer, Antonia Duncan, and other division heads gathered together at the company's headquarters to conduct the call. People who had just purchased large stakes in BET were on the line waiting to hear what Johnson had to say. Among them were Gordon Crawford, vice president of the mutual fund Capital Research Management, and Mario Gabelli, chairman of Gabelli & Company. Crawford and Gabelli were two of the most powerful managers of money invested in media and entertainment companies, and both now represented BET's largest institutional shareholders.

The call got under way with Johnson reiterating that the first-quarter results showed that the business was sound and growing. He explained that the subscriber revenues were based on the 27.5 million people who were paying for BET as part of their monthly cable bills. "We stand firmly in confidence that the numbers are accurate," he told to the people on the line.

Then, however, the analysts went on the attack.

"Are you losing viewers?" one analyst asked, sounding alarmed. "Yeah, wait a minute," another analyst quickly intoned. "You've been saying that you had 31.6 million subscribers and now you're only at 27.5 million? What happened to the gap?" The telephone line went silent.

Johnson and his executives scrambled quickly, and after several seconds the chief executive spoke up. Johnson explained that during the preparation for the public offering the company had been reporting its official Nielsen Media Research subscriber number. That figure, 31.6 million, included homes that were indeed receiving BET but were getting the channel on a free promotional basis for the first several months before then being required to pay. The 27.5 million subscribers, however, were already paying customers.

The explanation should have been sufficient. The free promotional periods were not uncommon in the cable industry. But BET's mishandling of the information left the investors rattled. Clear, precise communications were what Wall Street expected from companies, and Johnson and his staff had erred by not explaining the subscriber data from the outset.

But the BET executives were not the only people who were

treading in uncharted territory. The predominantly white Wall Street analysts and money managers who were now following BET had never dealt with a black-controlled company before. Johnson had now cleared the matter up, but it did not seem to matter to them. What they could have easily dismissed as a minor communications error they instead overreacted to. As if suddenly BET could not be trusted, when the conference call ended and BET resumed trading, investors continued dumping BET shares.

Over the next several days, BET stock lost much of its value, even dropping below its initial offering price. Devastated by the fiasco, Johnson consulted with Malone[5] about how to halt the exodus of investors. He telephoned Crawford and Gabelli, assuring them that the company was still sound and that there was no reason for alarm. Gabelli, who was based in Rye, New York, agreed to travel to Washington to meet with Johnson and Duncan. After the meeting, Gabelli decided that the "initial hiccups" had created an opportunity for his firm. Other money managers were turning their backs. It was as if they had decided to ignore the stock and "didn't want to do the research work to understand the company," Gabelli said. "And that was great for us."[6] His firm started buying more BET shares, and as the stock headed back up, Gabelli kept accumulating until he held 20 percent of BET's class A shares.

Although Johnson had quieted the immediate crisis, BET's days on Wall Street would never again be as smooth as those first few weeks. The incident was a harsh reinforcement of what Johnson knew when he undertook the public offering: As a public company, BET would be subject to skepticism and scrutiny from outsiders. He may have still controlled the votes, but privacy was now a thing of the past. Any problem or issues that might arise could no longer be quietly handled and swept away before people outside the executive suite ever learned about them. Now, federal laws required full disclosure of any matter that might affect value of the company, from Johnson's physical health to internal problems or scandalous behavior on the part of top executives.

And it was not long before problems and scandal hit.

In January 1992, Chickie Goodier, the first person Johnson had hired when he started BET, sued him and the company claiming she was owed over 500,000 shares of BET stock, which at the time would have been worth about $10 million. Vivian Goodier Roberts was now married and living in Nevada.

Two months later, another lawsuit hit. Carol Coody Jaafar and Johnson's sister, Paulette, respectively the second and third employees hired at the launch of BET, filed this one. They, too, claimed that they were owed millions in BET stock. Johnson and the women had signed agreements in 1980, giving them beneficial interests in shares of BET. The agreements stipulated that Johnson would "continue to hold at all times the legal title and right to vote such shares," and would be "listed as owner of such shares on the corporate record books."

But the three women who helped get BET off the ground claimed that Johnson and other company officials had ignored and improperly nullified the existence of their interests in Johnson's shares of BET. The women claimed that Johnson had "developed a scheme" to persuade them that their interests were worthless. The complaint charged that he "concealed from plaintiffs the true financial condition of BET with the intent and design to lull plaintiffs into the erroneous belief that their interest in BET was not worth anything . . . with the purpose and ultimate goal of keeping plaintiffs' shares for himself."[7]

Virgil Hemphill, who was BET's fourth employee, was contacted and asked to join the women in the lawsuit. Although he and Johnson no longer kept in touch much, Hemphill still felt a bond with his old college fraternity brother, and refused to become a plaintiff in the case. "Even though our friendship had ended, I'm not the kind to say he owed me a thing," Hemphill later said. "I didn't agree with some of the stuff he did, but Bobby had worked hard for that money."[8]

In response to the lawsuits, Johnson did not deny that the agreements existed. However, he contended that the women had forfeited their rights to the BET shares when they left the company and that they were now trying to capitalize on the years of sweat that he had put in after their departures.

As Johnson dug in and prepared to fight the lawsuits, the already frayed relationship with his sister got even nastier. In her court deposition, she accused him of "trying to drive me crazy through my family." She claimed that a few years earlier, when their mother—whom Johnson had by now moved into a nice, new home in Freeport, Illinois—came to Washington, Johnson had prevented her from seeing his sister, who also resided in Washington. "When he did that I felt rejected by Mother and it hurt me."

The two siblings were barely talking to each other, but they agreed to meet, Paulette said, because she wanted "to convince him to stop saying things and turning my mother against me."

So, Johnson and his sister sat down at a restaurant across the street from her Washington condominium. "Bobby," she started, "why are you turning Mother against me?"[9]

Johnson denied that he was doing such a thing. He made it clear that he had contacted their mother and other family members to inform them of his sister's apparently fragile emotional state. "I know you are hurting," Johnson told Paulette. Still, she says, he sternly warned her not to portray him as a bad guy to the family. "Polly," Johnson said, addressing his sister, "I tell you that you cannot win in this family. I will turn everyone against you."

According to family friends back in Johnson's hometown, he and Paulette and other family members would convene at a local hotel in Freeport for private, corporate-like "family meetings" designed to limit the damage caused by the warring siblings. But it would be a long time before Polly and Bobby would mend their rift.

Johnson vs. Johnson, as the legal case became known, went on for a few years and filled huge file boxes inside the U.S. District Court in Washington. Depositions were taken from the plaintiffs, Johnson, and even John Malone. Johnson eventually settled the lawsuits, paying the three women a total of $4 million. But the case cost Johnson even more. His marriage was dealt a blow when Chickie Goodier Roberts filed her complaint and in it revealed that she and Johnson had had a "personal relationship."

The news of Johnson's affair with Chickie caught Sheila by surprise. She knew nothing about it until she was subpoenaed in the legal case. "I had no idea this had been going on," Sheila Johnson later said, recalling that she and Goodier were always friendly and cordial. "I had been nice to her," she said. "And they had been having a *three-year* affair." Sheila said the words "three-year" a little louder and more slowly than her other words, emphasizing the amount of time that she had spent in the dark.[10] Just as Johnson was dealing with the lawsuits and the personal crisis that they had caused, more scandal hit the company.

On September 30, 1992, BET issued a terse statement announcing that Alan H. Nichols Jr., its vice president for corporate development and investor relations, had just been named executive vice president for finance and chief financial officer. Nichols, who was 33 years old at the time, was replacing Johnson's longtime trusted CFO, Antonia Duncan, who had suddenly resigned. A four-sentence story went out on the Dow Jones ticker to investors, saying that BET "declined to give the reason for Duncan's departure."

But as a public company, BET could not hide such details for long. Within days, rumors alleging that Duncan had embezzled money began to leak. When they released the company's quarterly results days later, BET officials acknowledged that they were investigating "financial irregularities" and even took a $700,000 charge "attributable to the unauthorized payment of goods and services that were not received by the BET Cable Network." The final cost would be much more.

What was revealed in the coming months was that Duncan, who was in her early forties and had been at the company for more than a decade, had been playing Johnson for a sucker, and he caught her in the act.

The always cost-conscious chief executive had noticed that Duncan, with her $170,000-a-year salary, seemed to be enjoying a rather lavish lifestyle. She was making major real estate purchases in Delaware and Virginia, and had even bought a restaurant. When she began to talk of buying another restaurant, Johnson became suspicious. He ordered an audit of BET's books and discovered that Duncan had been conducting an elaborate scheme right under his nose.

Beginning in 1988, Duncan set up six fictitious companies, five of them in Virginia and one in California. She opened a bank account for each company. Duncan also established a post office box for each company, making it appear that they were true businesses, when in fact her concocted firms—Video Broadcast, Atlantic Video, EBS Micro, LEP, Tele Video, and Production Concept—were nothing more than mail drops. She then created fake invoices and fake purchase orders. She presented prepared checks to pay the phony vendors, even having Johnson himself sign them. After the checks were deposited into the bank accounts of the fictitious companies, the funds were then transferred to Duncan's personal accounts. Before she was caught, her total take was $1.8 million.

According to other BET executives, Johnson was fond of Duncan and hurt by the deception. Even once he realized something was amiss, he was hesitant to press charges against Duncan and only wanted her to admit her wrongdoing and repay the money. In BET's earlier days, he may have indeed been able to handle such an issue quietly. But now the company was public, and Johnson was left with little choice in the matter. In the end, the government's case against Duncan was so strong that she waived indictment and pleaded guilty to interstate transportation of stolen property, and was sentenced to two and a half years in prison.

SHAKIN' IT . . . SMACKIN' IT

With its stock trading publicly, cash flowing, and profile growing, BET was perfectly prepared to move into the 1990s. The timing could not have been better. Around the country, a cultural revolution was in progress as the whole hip-hop movement began to infiltrate the music, fashion, and style of an entire generation. A new class of young, black multimillionaire athletes and entertainers was taking shape, and they were cocksure, full of swagger and confidence. As this phenomenon gained momentum, BET was right there, and the network became the place where all of America could witness the cultural shift on a daily basis.

This was years before hard-edged rappers like Nelly or 50 Cent could even dream of appearing on the *Tonight Show with Jay Leno*. A musician did not need "crossover" appeal to get on BET. Many artists and their videos first appeared on BET, and then the performers used that platform to gain widespread popularity. As in the network's early days, when it helped rap and hip-hop pioneers like Kurtis Blow and Run-DMC gain national prominence, BET continued to play a major role in introducing new acts. Early releases from future superstars like Mary J. Blige, R. Kelly, and Boyz II Men first appeared on BET. Mariah Carey, who became one of the top selling artists of all time, sat for her first nationally televised interview on BET.

BET became a powerful influence on the culture and the entire music industry. Suddenly, professional athletes, like basketball star Shaquille O'Neal and football sensation Deion Sanders, wanted to be rappers on the side. The exposure BET gave rap music powered the fortunes of young moguls like Russell Simmons and Sean "P-Diddy" Combs, who became so successful that they expanded their music businesses into clothing lines and restaurants.

Johnson, who had set out only to build a successful cable enterprise, was now also becoming one of the most powerful figures in black music. And it wasn't long before he was flexing his muscles.

MTV for several years had been paying record labels to gain the exclusive rights to videos when they were first released. This meant that for the first few weeks of release, the only place to see a new video was MTV. These exclusive deals meant that MTV, which had many more subscribers and far more ad revenue than BET, was essentially paying for videos that the record labels were gladly providing for free. It enabled MTV to maintain its superiority over the field of fledgling competitors, such as the interactive channel, The Box. But it had had little impact on BET because MTV had never played much black music anyway.

But by the early 1990s, the white rock and pop genres that MTV favored were growing stale. Meanwhile, R&B and rap acts were beginning to flourish, and more and more black artists were having crossover appeal for white listeners. In the summer of 1991, when MCA Records released a new video for the single "Now That We've Found Love" by the rap act Heavy D & the Boyz, Johnson was incensed when he learned that his music programming people were denied a copy of the video because MTV had locked up exclusive rights. MTV, which had a subscriber base about twice the size of BET's and annual revenue several times larger, was now trying to use its muscle to snatch BET's business.

This was predatory, as Johnson saw it. And he was not about to let MTV move in on his turf. Immediately, he called Ernie Singleton, who was in charge of MCA's black music division at the time. "Since you value us so little," Johnson told Singleton, who was based in Los Angeles, "let's just take the rest of your artists off BET." And so it was. For the next couple of weeks MCA artists who had current videos, such as Pebbles, Ralph Tresvant, and Gladys Knight, disappeared from BET's video rotation. Johnson knew that most black acts needed BET, since MTV was interested in only a select few black videos. "We are absolutely opposed to music video exclusivity," Johnson told the *Washington Post.* "We feel it's anti-competitive, anti-consumer and not in the best interest of the cable industry."[1] A couple of weeks later the boycott ended when Johnson convinced MCA to avoid such exclusive deals in the future.

It was ironic that music videos had become so important to Johnson that he would fight so vociferously for them. After all, several years earlier when BET was a new, fledgling entity, Johnson had been reluctant to devote much of his programming to videos.

In the early 1980s, when BET and MTV were just getting started, some black artists were dismayed that MTV refused to play their videos. But MTV executives insisted that, just as radio stations had specific music formats, their new music channel was an outlet only for pure rock and roll. The black funk star Rick James in 1982 became an outspoken critic of MTV after the network rejected the videos for his singles "Super Freak" and "Give It to Me Baby."[2]

Even though its early programming was exclusionary, MTV enjoyed rapid success and demonstrated that its experimental music video format worked well on cable television. The videos were great promotional material for the record labels, and the cable network was quickly becoming as important an outlet as radio for promoting new releases. But by refusing to air black videos, MTV created a clear opportunity for someone. And with BET as the only black cable channel, that someone was Bob Johnson.

With the whole racial exclusion issue swirling around MTV, Johnson met with some of his executives and partners at a cable convention in southern California. "Bob, you ought to seize this opportunity to start showing more black videos," suggested Don Anderson, the Time Inc. executive who was in charge of HBO's investment in BET. "It's free programming and it's high-quality programming."[3]

Johnson, however, was resistant. He did not want his channel to become dominated by videos. BET was already showing a half hour of videos each week on *Video Soul*, and he felt that that was enough. Instead of music, he wanted BET to develop more highbrow and thoughtful public-service-oriented programming.

"We don't want to be a video channel," he said. "Music will cheapen the product." But with 24 hours a day to fill and few decent and affordable choices of available programming, Johnson was eventually convinced that following MTV's lead was the most prudent course he could take.

"One of the smartest things that ever happened was to walk right through that door that MTV left open," says Jeff Lee, whose first responsibility when he was hired in 1982 was to begin expanding BET's music video programming.

Later that year, Michael Jackson broke the color barrier on MTV when CBS Records released his "Thriller" album. The video for the single, "Billie Jean," was so unlike anything that the rock and roll devotees at MTV had ever seen, they gave in and put it on the air. Quickly followed by "Beat It" and "Thriller" videos, the Michael Jackson productions were so revolutionary that they forever changed the music video world. The videos helped turn "Thriller" into the top-selling album of all time with

40 million copies sold worldwide. And MTV, which had pledged its devotion to rock, had now gone black, and there was no going back. Still, it would be several years before MTV would show much interest in many of the same artists that BET aired.

For BET, the video format was so lucrative that Johnson and Lee kept adding more and more music programming. By 1991, 42 percent of BET's programming was music videos. Five years later, in 1996, over 60 percent of the network's schedule was filled with music videos. There was also news, public affairs, gospel music, and sitcoms. But for the most part, BET was all about music videos. And with the videos generating generous profit margins, Johnson was converted.

He dropped his once high-minded vision of sophisticated programming and instead began singing the virtues of music videos. People began to ask him: "Why is BET showing so many videos?" And Johnson began to remind people that the "E" in BET stood for entertainment, and music was one of the most popular forms of entertainment in the black community. "Music is a cultural expression," he would repeat, over and over again. "It is the dominant art form in black America."

But as rap music developed into its hard-core "gangsta" style, the videos that were being shipped to BET were increasingly racy and provocative—filled with images of sex, violence, alcohol and drugs, flashy cars and jewelry, and scantily clad women. Johnson and his programming heads at first refused to air the gangsta rap videos.

Soon, though, BET was the principal purveyor of the hard-core videos. Teenagers came home from school and turned on BET to view a steady stream of these images. It was not long before the network began to gain a reputation for the raunchy fare.

Young people were tuning in en masse, but black professionals and leaders in the black community criticized the proliferation of the hard-edged videos. At cocktail parties, in office cafeterias, or at the beauty shop—wherever the topic of BET came up, the response was often the same: It was becoming demeaning and embarrassing. "BET is the only thing that black people have on television, and it's gotten to the point that you don't want to come home and turn it on," said Tom Joyner, the popular nationally syndicated radio host. "Nobody comes in the house and says, 'I can't wait to turn on BET.' If you have your pastor over you are sure not going to turn it on. And if you have white friends over you're not going to say, 'Hey, you need to check out our BET.' I've been inside Bob's office and he doesn't even have it on in there.' "[4]

Indeed, inside BET's executive suite the network's evolving reputation was causing consternation. Executives found themselves trying to defend the network to their friends and to people that BET did business with. When Johnson and his head of affiliate sales, Curtis Symonds, traveled to Philadelphia to negotiate a new contract with the cable giant Comcast Corporation, the company's chief executive, Brian Roberts, did not hesitate to express his opinion of BET's programming. "I don't like the way your channel looks," Roberts told them. In what Symonds recalls as a "nasty" exchange, Johnson assured Roberts that BET's programming would improve.

Even the BET executives themselves sometimes found it hard to hide their own dissatisfaction with the network. In 1997, BET's vice president for programming, Lydia Cole, spoke at a music industry conference and admitted to the audience that she did not allow her own daughters to watch the channel. "We don't watch BET," Cole said. "I'm concerned about the images portrayed of young girls."[5] After her comments, Cole became persona non grata around the network. She soon resigned.

During executive meetings, Johnson was urged to spend more money to offset the negative videos with more original programming. Just as he had told Roberts, he promised his staff that over time, more meaningful programming would be produced. But he also constantly reminded them that their main priority was to generate profits for the company's shareholders. And the video programming was serving that purpose well. "We don't need to reinvent the wheel," Johnson told them. "We just need to paint it black."[6]

Johnson's primary business partner, John Malone, stayed out of sight and out of any controversy that the network's programming was generating. Malone did, after all, have a clause in his original investment agreement stating that BET's "programming shall conform to the ordinary standards of good taste and decency prevailing in the communities in which BET serves." But Malone showed little concern that the raunchy and violent videos may have been stretching the boundaries of decency.

Malone trusted Johnson's judgment, and he left him alone to run the company. He was the perfect partner, more mentor than manager, offering his guidance and advice—especially on matters pertaining to financing and capital markets—but never trying to pull any strings inside the company's operations. "It can't be a white company serving a black marketplace," Malone told a television interviewer.[7] "It has to be a black company, black controlled, black managed, and part of the black community if it's going to be a meaningful voice in that community."

With Malone, Johnson had access not only to the most dominant person in the cable industry, but also to one of the true financial wizards of American business. As *Forbes* magazine calculated, an investor who made a $100 purchase of TCI stock when Malone joined the company in 1973, then followed every move that Malone made—spin-offs, trades, and so on—had by 1999 realized a profit of $181,100.[8]

With his home and company based in Denver, Malone showed up around BET only for annual meetings, and he was in the door and out before shareholders hardly noticed. When the board met privately, recalls fellow board member Herb Wilkins, "Malone would come to meetings, listen to Bob and say, 'It sounds good to me.' And then he would leave."

Nevertheless, with Malone in the background, there was still the lingering misperception that he was a puppet master, pulling all of the strings. Johnson, skeptics continued to assert, was "fronting for the white man."

Johnson's other large equity partner, however, was beginning to question its ongoing involvement in BET. Ever since the 1991 merger of Time Inc. and Warner Communications Inc. that had created the media behemoth known as Time Warner, the firm had been saddled with a huge debt load. By 1994, Time Warner had $14.5 billion in revenues, but $15 billion in long-term debt. In stepped Richard D. Parsons, a Time Warner board member and chief executive of the New York–based Dime Savings Bank.

A burly six-foot-four man with a teddy bear demeanor that masked a grizzly bear's soul, Parsons was named president of Time Warner, the company's second-highest job. Gerald Levin, Time Warner's chief executive, assigned Parsons to take a look at all of the many businesses that Time Warner was in, and figure out what could be done to reduce the company's debt.

Compared to the company's premium portfolio of properties—*Time* magazine, HBO, Warner Brothers Studios—the small profit BET was generating was not significant. But Time Warner had gotten its 15 percent stake in BET for little or no cost way back in the early 1980s when HBO first gave the fledgling BET satellite time and sales and management expertise. So anything that Time Warner got for selling its stake in BET would be pure profit.

Parsons, an African-American, grappled with whether the company should try to maintain its relationship with the black network. Like other entertainment companies, Time Warner was concerned with targeting African-American consumers. But at the same time, Time Warner was also facing strong public pressure because of some of the violent gangsta videos that its Warner Music unit was distributing. The last thing that Parsons needed was for BET's risqué video lineup to add to Time Warner's headaches.

What also concerned Parsons was that the quality of the BET network did not seem to be showing much improvement. "We can't figure out what Bob is going to do with the network," Parsons said. "Is it going to get better?"[9] Parsons and Levin decided to sever the partnership. On November 2, 1995, Time Warner agreed to sell its 3,036,600 BET shares back to BET Holdings Inc., for $19.10 per share, or a total price of $58 million. This placed an implied value of $390 million on all of BET Holdings. Time Warner had made a nice profit on its BET investment. But just two years later, the BET stock would be worth $63 per share. Parsons and Levin, had they hung in a little bit longer, would have picked up an additional $133 million to add to Time Warner's coffers. "They made a bad mistake, a bad, bad mistake," Johnson later said emphatically. "I tried to talk them into staying, but they were looking for anything they could get to pay down the debt."

By the time that BET reached its 20th anniversary in 2000, Johnson had fully embraced music videos. Nearly 70 percent of the network's programming was music related, and music accounted for 80 percent of the company's annual cash flow—or earnings before interest, taxes, depreciation, and amortization—which totaled about $150 million. The mutually beneficial relationship between BET and the record labels ran deep, with each of them now dependent on the other and hundreds of people employed on both sides to keep the music video pipeline filled with product.

But despite the success, Johnson received few accolades for what BET had become, and this frustrated him deeply. He complained that MTV, which was similarly thriving on a steady diet of pernicious programming, was receiving heaps of praise while BET was garnering plenty of criticism. "If people would just judge BET for what it is instead of what they'd like it to be," Johnson moaned. "But nobody will sing our praises."[10]

There were some, however, who were singing BET's praises. To commemorate the network's 20 years in business, the independent label Tommy Boy Records, which produced many of the salacious rap music videos that were generating controversy and criticism, ran a full-page ad in the *Hollywood Reporter*. The page, depicting a woman's big, brown, bare-bottomed derriere, read: "Congratulations BET! You keep on shakin' it, we'll keep on smackin' it."

"TIRED OL' RERUNS"

J efferi Lee and Ed Gordon, BET's top news anchor, sat back and tried to relax as their flight lifted off from the freezing January cold of Washington and headed for the West Coast. But the Los Angeles–bound plane had hardly reached its cruising altitude before the two men started arguing.

Gordon, the buttery-smooth anchor of the daily *BET News* show, had over the past few years displayed a real mastery of one-on-one interviews. On his program *Conversations with Ed Gordon*, he had conducted lengthy close-ups with major newsmakers such as President George H.W. Bush and the Nation of Islam leader, Louis Farrakhan. When Washington, D.C., mayor Marion Barry Jr. was imprisoned for illegal drug use, Gordon traveled to the federal penitentiary in western Pennsylvania to score the first interview granted by Barry after becoming an inmate.

Gordon was unflappable on the air and the consummate newsman. But behind the cameras if he was agitated or pushed in a direction that he didn't want to go, the truculent side of the Detroit native would emerge. This, joked one colleague, was "when the Detroit would come out of Ed." Such was the case as Gordon and Lee faced off over how to handle what was awaiting them when the plane touched down: BET's biggest news coup ever—an exclusive interview with the football legend O.J. Simpson following his acquittal in the brutal murders of his former wife, Nicole Brown Simpson, and her friend, Ron Goldman.

For three months since the stunning jury verdict that had set Simpson free and ignited the nation, giving rise to racially polarizing debates, every news organization in the United States and many beyond its borders had been clamoring to talk with the gridiron star. The venerable NBC News appeared to have the Simpson interview all locked up, and the star anchor of the *Today* show, the pert Katie Couric, was preparing to lead a team of the network's correspondents who would pepper Simpson with questions as much of the nation tuned in.

But Johnson, along with others at BET, personally contacted Simpson and his lawyer, Johnnie Cochran, to pitch the idea of having the former football star address the country on the nation's only black television channel.

What persuaded Simpson to award the coveted interview to BET was a side deal that Johnson and Lee had cut. Following his acquittal, Simpson had produced a mail-order video with his version of what happened at the bloody Brentwood murder scene. If Simpson would agree to do the interview on BET, Johnson and Lee said, they would then run paid advertisements for the $30 video at the commercial breaks during the interview.

Gordon was not happy about the video deal. Major news organizations were already being dismissive of BET's ability to conduct a tough and thorough interview. In the days following the verdict, polls showed that blacks overwhelming believed that Simpson was innocent, while most whites felt he had gotten away with murder. The feeling was that for BET to snatch the interview away from NBC and other major networks, they must have been promising to give Simpson a friendly forum. The implication was that a black reporter could not look at the issue impartially. No one had ever raised such concerns about a white reporter's ability to be fair. Such sentiments were an attack on Gordon's credibility as a journalist, so he was especially sensitive about how the video advertisements would be perceived.

"This is going to be a problem," he insisted to Lee. "It will impugn my integrity."

"Look, Bob and I cut the deal," Lee retorted. "The deal is done."

But Gordon did not give up. After they arrived in Los Angeles and Johnson was consulted, Johnson and Lee placated Gordon by deciding not to air the ads for the video during the hour-long interview. Instead, the advertisements for the video would appear at the beginning of the show and at the end.

The live, televised interview took place on January 24, 1996. Most of the media world had been dismissive of BET's ability to interview Simpson, but one never would have guessed it based on the hordes of reporters who camped out at BET's Burbank studio to cover Simpson's arrival and departure. Simpson had been avoiding the media since the trial ended and did not want to be bombarded before and after the interview. Lee saw this as a perfect opportunity to have some fun and get back at the mainstream media for disrespecting BET.

He had the show's producer, Curtis Gadson, rent studio space at a nearby facility and hire a local production crew to prepare the set. Satellite trucks, cameras, and reporters camped outside BET's studio waiting for Simpson to arrive. There were also some reporters who, expecting a possible change in venue, were waiting at Simpson's home and planning to follow his limousine as it pulled out of the gated property. To throw them off the trail, Gadson and Lee hired three limousines, which pulled out at the same time and headed in three different directions.

Meanwhile, the production crew that Gadson had hired arrived at the secretive studio a couple of hours before airtime. But when the crew, who were white, learned that they were going to be working on an O.J. Simpson interview, they grabbed their equipment and left in protest. Gadson and a few other BET employees stepped in and raced to get the set ready.

When the car carrying Simpson arrived, it was all alone, as none of the media had managed to keep up. And with the paint still drying on the wall behind him, the former football star spoke about the murder case that had captivated the nation.

Simpson had not testified during his highly publicized trial, so the world was anxious to hear what he had to say. During the interview, Gordon's questions were tough and straightforward. But Simpson was not so forthcoming with his answers. When Gordon asked him where he was on the night of the murders, Simpson refused to answer, instead urging viewers to order his tape to get the answer.

The event was deemed a tremendous success for BET. The interview delivered the highest rating ever in the history of the network, scoring a 6.2 Nielsen rating, meaning that 6.2 percent of television households in the United States that could receive BET tuned in. This translated to a total of 3.1 million cable households and 4.2 million viewers.[1] It was three times the average audience for a typical cable show, and one of the highest-rated shows in the history of cable. Not only did the network gain credibility as a news organization as a result of the Simpson interview, but also Gordon was suddenly "discovered." His national profile expanded, and soon thereafter he was hired away by NBC as an anchor and reporter, mainly on the MSNBC news network. A few years later, when his NBC contract expired, he returned to BET. Before the O.J. interview, Gordon's fundamental competency as a journalist had been questioned. Afterward, the only question that the major networks were asking was "Why didn't we hire this guy a long time ago?"

Just as being the only black-oriented channel on television helped BET nab the O.J. interview, it also helped the network in countless other instances.

BET's niche was blackness. Whether it involved breaking news about black people, sitcoms with black stars, or black-oriented talk shows, if it was of special interest to black people it was perfect for BET's programming format. The groundbreaking NBC soap opera *Generations*, which had a predominantly black cast, found a second home on BET during the early 1990s. And when major network shows like *Benson*, *227*, and *Roc* were canceled by the big broadcasters, their reruns were purchased by BET.

There were also original shows that likely never would have found their way onto television without BET. Public affairs programs like *For Black Men Only* and *Our Voices* convened panels to discuss issues vital to the black community. The children's program *Story Porch* used stars like Bill Cosby and Maya Angelou to read African-American folktales to an audience of young people. And there was *Teen Summit*, which never made much money but kept going strong because Sheila Johnson convinced Kaiser Permanente and the Centers for Disease Control to sponsor the show.

The beauty of BET's network programming was that nothing or no one from the mainstream media world could dictate what was important to its audience. "It was great to have that media ownership," says Jefferi Lee, who headed programming. "We could say to the rest of the world, 'It doesn't matter whether something is important to you. It's important to our audience.'" When Ron Brown, the U.S. secretary of commerce, was tragically killed in a plane crash in 1996, BET did more than just cover the news like all the major networks were doing. Feeling that Brown's death had an especially profound impact on the black community, BET devoted six continuous hours of programming to the memorial service. Several months earlier, on October 16, 1995, when the Million Man March convened in Washington, not only did BET cover the march, but Johnson shut down the company's offices so employees

Raised in rural Mississippi and in the factory town of Freeport, Illinois, Robert Johnson excelled in his classes at Freeport High School. Upon graduation in 1964, he enrolled at the University of Illinois, and was the only one among the 10 children in his family to attend college. (Photo courtesy of *The Journal Standard,* Freeport, Illinois.)

Johnson (shown circa 1980) quit his job, took out a $15,000 bank loan, and in August 1979 announced the creation of Black Entertainment Television. (Photo courtesy of The Cable Center.)

In this 1980 photo, taken within months of BET's launch, Johnson and two of his first employees, Virgil Hemphill (*left*) and Vivian Goodier (*center*), are shown standing in front of the network's homemade, glue-and-poster-board exhibit. (Photo courtesy of The Cable Center.)

Johnson with the film and television actress Sheryl Lee Ralph at a 1988 cable industry event. (Photo courtesy of The Cable Center.)

Bob and Sheila Johnson attending the Cable Ace Awards in 1992. (Photo courtesy of The Cable Center.)

Johnson with BET's president and chief operating officer, Debra Lee, in 1997.
(Photo courtesy of The Cable Center.)

In a 1996 photo taken at the company's Washington headquarters are many of the executives who helped build BET: (*left to right*) Curtis Symonds, Janis Thomas, Sheila Crump Johnson, James Ebron, Jefferi Lee, and William Gordon. Johnson eventually forced most of them to leave the company—even his own wife, Sheila. (*Photo credit*: Welton B. Doby III.)

HELLO and a hearty salute to Bob Johnson and BET, who recently proclaimed that BET does more to serve the Black community each and every day than the creator of this feature — one "playa hating" Aaron McGruder — has done his entire life.

In order to follow the fine example set by Mr. Johnson, we present to you, the reader, in the spirit of Black uplift —

a black woman's gyrating rear end.

From now on, when you think "black women's gyrating rear ends," don't just think BET, think "The Boondocks."

And thank you, Bob Johnson, for shining your light for the rest of us to follow!

"The Boondocks" comic strips, which appear in more than 250 newspapers, made BET a routine target of satirical criticism. This 2000 strip was banned from some newspapers because of its salacious nature. (Boondocks © 2000 Aaron McGruder. Dist. by Universal Press Syndicate. Reprinted with permission. All rights reserved.)

Johnson attending the Fourth Annual Wall Street Project Conference shown here with (*from left to right*) Richard Grasso (then NYSE chairman), Johnson, Viacom chief Sumner Redstone, Reverend Jesse Jackson, and Citicorp chairman and CEO Sanford Weill (*photo*: © Ciniglio Lorenzo/Corbis Sygma). Above, Johnson's longtime business partner, John Malone of Liberty Media (*photo*: © Maiman Rick/Corbis Sygma).

On December 18, 2002, the National Basketball Association awarded Johnson with the right to purchase the league's new Charlotte, North Carolina, franchise. Here, the new owner and his son meet the New York media inside the NBA store on Fifth Avenue. *Left to right*: NBA deputy commissioner Russ Granik, NBA board of governors head and Phoenix Suns owner Jerry Colangelo, NBA commissioner David Stern, Johnson, Brett Johnson, and Charlotte mayor Pat McCrory. (*Photo credit*: Ron Antonelli.)

could attend and took out a full-page ad in *USA Today* supporting the event.

There was no other television outlet competing with BET, so practically every original programming project it pursued was something unique. Johnson would often remind his staff of this. "We are the only unicorn in the forest," he would tell them.[2]

As with the O.J. interview, the network was able to take advantage of its unique position to gain exclusive news programming opportunities. Viewers knew that when a significant news event involving black people occurred and all the major news organizations were covering the story, they could turn to BET to get the "black perspective." Gordon's 1994 exclusive interview with Farrakhan was conducted in response to Khalid Muhammad, the Nation of Islam spokesman who had just set off a firestorm around the country with his controversial remarks about Jews, calling them "bloodsuckers." And in 1991 when four Los Angeles police officers were acquitted in the beating of Rodney King, BET ran special programming examining the surprising court verdict, in addition to Gordon's exclusive interview with President Bush after his return from examining the devastation caused by the postverdict riots.

These kinds of events created exceptional programming opportunities for BET, and the shows helped to enhance the affection many black Americans had developed for the network. But for the many viewers who had hoped that BET would become a round-the-clock sophisticated arbiter of all things good for the race, it soon became clear that they were sadly mistaken. Johnson's priority was profits, and he decided that his continued success in television would come from keeping the schedule filled with cheap programming that would appeal to the masses. As Malone had told him from the outset, "Keep your costs down."

And Johnson was determined to do just that, even though it was beginning to make him unpopular. Looking behind the scenes at how in-house shows were produced was like pulling the curtain back and revealing the feeble wizard in Oz. Employees were griping and fighting to get things that were basic amenities at other television outlets, like blank tapes or a well-organized library of past shows. News programs, such as *BET News with Ed Gordon* and *Tonight with Tavis Smiley*, were done on budgets so lean that they sometimes would run out midway through the season. It led to Smiley and Johnson developing a contentious relationship, as the fast-rising talk show star constantly needled Johnson about improving the quality of programming.

The more raunchy the videos and other tasteless programming the network showed, the more some people in the black community would complain. For example, the variety show *Live from L.A.* included a sketch called "Bitch Please," which made fun of women who claim that they've been assaulted by black celebrities. *Newsweek* reported that the black actress Pam Grier was so offended when the same show aired a skit called "Pimps and Hos" that she tried to cancel a planned appearance on the program.[3]

In Canada, where many of that country's more than 600,000 black people had lobbied to get BET carried on their cable systems, viewers expressed disgust at what they saw when they tuned in. In a *Toronto Globe and Mail* article, critic Vernon Clement Jones described a couple of typical BET moments such as a video in which "a black girl crawls across a bar counter, her large breasts barely contained by a bikini top," and a video program with a host who does a segment on the streets in which he is shown "asking white folks in D.C. to eat his 'booger.'" As one Canadian viewer told Jones, "BET came here invoking black solidarity to get the support of local blacks. When it had our backing, it abandoned us and then bombarded us with jive-talk images."[4]

Back in the United States, black leaders were reaching out to appeal to Johnson about some of the images on the network. In 2001, a group of leaders from national black fraternities and sororities met with Johnson to discuss their concerns about BET's programming. In the meeting, he told the leaders of the Greek organizations the same thing that he always told people who tried to convince him to change the network's format: BET is a business, Johnson told them politely. And that's how he would continue to run it.[5]

Why should BET's business model be burdened by a need to be socially redeeming? Johnson would ask. Its cable brother MTV showed plenty of raunchy videos also, but no one was complaining about that channel. To be sure, Johnson understood that because BET was the only black channel, the expectations for it were far broader than anyone had for MTV. But he refused to let those expectations affect his bottom line. "We can not be all things to all people," he said.

Many people, including executives inside BET, tried to tell Johnson that he could make plenty of money and at the same time make more viewers happy. But alas, no one around the BET founder could convince him that broad, uplifting programming and profits were not mutually exclusive.

Johnson was, just as he had been throughout his life, stubborn and singularly focused about how he wanted to run his network. No one could change his view. As Debra Tang, a vice president in programming, reminded her colleagues countless times: "This is Bob Johnson's sandbox."[6]

Even Johnson's own wife disagreed with his view that BET harbored no extra burden or responsibility to show uplifting programs. Because of Sheila, the issues show *Teen Summit* survived season after season, although it did little to help the bottom line. Such shows received low ratings, but Sheila believed that the company had to be willing to take a financial

hit in order to use its powerful forum to help inform and em-
power its viewers.

Her husband did not budge, though. "The E in BET," he told
people, "stands for entertainment." However, the unfortunate
joke that began making the rounds was that BET stood for "Bad
Entertainment Television." As one of the network's longtime on-
air stars put it, "Bob chose profit over quality."

Beyond music, Johnson found another cheap form of entertainment: comedy. The music videos were the driving force behind the network, but its most successful show became
ComicView, a low-budget program featuring undiscovered, struggling stand-up comedians performing before live audiences.

The show provided a platform for some comedians who
would go on to major success. D. L. Hughley, the star of movies
and television sitcoms, was the first host of ComicView. And
Cedric "The Entertainer" Kyles also worked on the show early in
his career. The humor on the show was mostly off-color—the
backroom, salty style that had made black comics like Redd
Foxx, Moms Mabley, and Richard Pryor famous on the comedy
club circuit before they hit the mainstream. Just like in the music
videos, words were sometimes bleeped out and vulgar images
were blurred.

Indeed, the material was sometimes out of bounds. On one
occasion, one of Farrakhan's sons sat in the audience as the show
was being taped in Los Angeles. Aware that he and other Nation
of Islam members were present, the comedian started making
jokes about eating pork: "If Farrakhan tried to get between me
and a pork chop, I'd eat the pork chop and spit the bone on Farrakhan." The audience cracked up. That is, except for Farrakhan's
son and the Nation of Islam members who were accompanying
him. After the taping, the wisecracking comedian was attacked
outside the studio and severely beaten.

Within days, Farrakhan traveled to meet with Johnson at
BET's headquarters in Washington. He explained that he was

sorry for what had happened to the comedian, but he had no control over the violent response that the attempt at comedy elicited. Besides, the powerful minister added, "The comic should really be more careful about what he says."[7]

For many people, watching *ComicView* was a guilty pleasure—publicly, they feigned disdain for the lowbrow show, but privately many of them tuned in to, as the show's opening theme song said, "get your laugh on." By the mid-1990s it was BET's top-rated show, airing for 11 hours per week and drawing an average audience of 450,000 viewers.

And what Johnson liked best about *ComicView* was that it was a dirt-cheap production. It looked low-budget, and it was low-budget. The total cost to produce an hour-long *ComicView* show was about $18,500. By comparison, an "inexpensive" half-hour television sitcom runs about $500,000 an episode, and a network hit like NBC's *Friends* costs over $6 million for each half-hour episode.

The economics of *ComicView* provide a perfect illustration of how adept Johnson was at squeezing value out of every penny he invested. While everyone else in Hollywood was shooting a maximum of one show per day, BET saved dramatically on production costs by pushing workers to shoot four episodes of *ComicView* in one day. Over the course of a year, the network would shoot a total of 65 to 80 episodes, and then slice and dice outtakes from those shows to create another 40 episodes. Most telling of all was the paycheck that the comedians received: $150 per appearance.

As Curtis Gadson, the show's executive producer and former chief of entertainment programming at BET, explains, "The show was designed to give a chance to comics who would not be seen anywhere else. We gave them a forum."

But that reasoning wasn't good enough once the comics realized that the network was airing multiple replays from each appearance they made on the show with no residual payments for the comedians. In 1999, Gadson received a telephone call from an official of the American Federation of Television and Radio Artists (AFTRA), a union that represents entertainers. Three of the union's representatives asked to meet Gadson for lunch to try to convince him to increase the rate that BET was paying the comedians. Johnson had always fought to keep unions out of BET, and Gadson knew as much. Still, he agreed to the lunch.

"How about we meet at a restaurant in Beverly Hills?" one union rep said to Gadson. "No, let's meet at M&M Soul Food in Pasadena," Gadson suggested. "If you want to talk with me about black people, you need to know about black people. So, we're going to eat collard greens, black-eyed peas, and chicken."

During the down-home meal, the three union representatives—two white men and a black women—told Gadson of their concern that the rate BET was paying comics was too low. A more reasonable amount would be $500 to $800 per appearance, they suggested. Gadson balked, feeling that the union officials simply did not understand that *ComicView* was giving black comedians an opportunity for exposure that was worth far more than their meager paychecks. "When you go and complain to all of the television shows that don't even hire black comedians, then we can continue talking," he told them. With that, the lunch ended abruptly—before the union reps could even try the sweet potato pie.

This exchange was only the beginning of an increasingly heated debate. Several days later, AFTRA took out a full-page advertisement in the Hollywood trade journal *Variety*. Designed to embarrass BET into submission, the ad was an open letter to Johnson requesting negotiations to increase fees and benefits for the comics. "Paying a onetime appearance fee of $150 without residuals while the performance reruns on your network for years is grossly unfair," the letter read. "Comics are embarrassed to report that they are even forced to pay their own travel and lodging expenses." But what gave the ad so much credibility was that more than 100 comedians, including major stars like Jay Leno, Richard Pryor, and Marsha Warfield, signed it.

Overnight, throughout the entertainment and cable industry, the advertisement became news itself. What began as a criticism of compensation for comics evolved into a critique of the entire network. Instantly, the once-muted carping about the quality of BET's programming grew loud and gained credibility—if such reputable entertainers as Pryor and Leno were publicly complaining about the network, then there must really be a serious problem, observers figured.

For the black people who had treated BET like family—never publicly airing their dirty laundry—it was a liberating moment. D. L. Hughley, who at the time was starring in his own ABC sitcom, *The Hughleys*, was quoted in *Newsweek* griping about his former employer. "If a mainstream company were treating black people the way BET has and is, it would've been a big mess long before now," he told the magazine. "Because it's black people mistreating black people, everyone's been hesitant to speak up. But wrong is wrong."[8] The filmmaker Spike Lee, while attending a press event for his stand-up feature, *The Original Kings of Comedy*, which starred former *ComicView* hosts Hughley and Cedric the Entertainer, was asked by a reporter, "Why is MTV producing this film, and not BET?" Lee's curt response was witty and biting: "Because we didn't want to be paid in sandwiches," he told the reporter.[9]

Back in Washington, Johnson and his senior executives went into crisis management mode. The company took out its own ads in *Variety* and in the *Hollywood Reporter*, rebutting AFTRA's charge. Johnson's friend and business partner, Butch Lewis, went on the air on BET defending the network and urging viewers to rally around Johnson. Johnson wrote letters to the heads of some of the major cable companies responsible for distributing BET, seeking to reassure them that there was no need for concern. In his October 25, 1999, letter to Leo Hindery, who at the time was chief executive of Time Warner Cable, Johnson wrote:

> There have been a few instances of negative press surrounding our company, as of late, and I just wanted to take time to address concern that you might have now, as a result of some issues that have been raised. . . . We feel that our treatment of the comedians that appear on our network is fair. In addition to payment that they receive for appearing, these performers are given their first opportunities to advance their careers through the national exposure that they receive from being on BET. Exposure that they would not have access to otherwise. Secondly, there have been questions raised about our commitment to providing high quality programming on BET. We feel this criticism is not entirely justified.[10]

To confront the onslaught of criticism, Johnson issued to his senior executives an internal memo of "talking points." This provided them with thoughtful and precise answers to the questions that everyone was asking. As one of the questions and answers illustrates, it was like following a script:

> Q: Many are saying BET is "pimping" its black talent. How do you feel about this statement?

> A: First of all, to use the term "pimping" implies there are illegal, forceful tactics being used to coerce someone to do their job. When you are trying to get your career started in the entertainment world, your options are limited. And when you are African American, those options are even fewer. We offer people an opportunity to perform on BET, and people decide on their own whether or not they want to perform. We continue to receive support from all of our talent, writers, producers, directors, and the many associates who work for BET year after year.[11]

By the time that the *ComicView* debate settled down, AFTRA had issued a "no contract, no work" order, urging comics to stop appearing on the show. BET moved the production across the country to Atlanta, where there was a strong supply of hungry black comics who were less experienced and did not have membership in the union. And the pay for comics on the show did eventually increase to $300 per appearance, still short of the amount the union was demanding.

Johnson already had gained a reputation as being antiunion for his resistance to BET production workers who earlier had tried to organize. In the mid-1990s the National Labor Relations Board ruled that BET had illegally threatened to fire production employees who voted to join the International Brotherhood of Electrical Workers. Johnson denied that he or his management had done such a thing.[12]

As in the previous case, he had again avoided signing a collective bargaining agreement. He conceded very little to the actors' union, and even though he agreed to have workers connected to one of his shows, *Live from L.A.*, work under the terms of a labor pact, he did it by using Butch Lewis as an independent producer for the show, thus leaving BET itself without any liability to the union.

ComicView was the source of some embarrassment for executives at the network, but the economic formula was too strong to change it. "They were ashamed of *ComicView*," says the show's longtime executive producer, Curtis Gadson. "It was making more money than any other show and they were ashamed of it." Gadson, who eventually became BET's senior vice president of entertainment programming, was later fired over production disputes and disagreements with Debra Lee.

As a result of the *ComicView* dilemma, Johnson stayed on the defensive. In the media and in conversations with industry people, he insisted that BET's ability to produce original programming was limited by its economic paradigm. The company was certainly profitable, but not to the extent of comparable channels, he argued. It was not fair to compare how BET compensated its talent with the level of compensation paid at other channels because there was an ongoing lack of parity in cable subscriber fees and advertising rates. For example, MTV was receiving an average of 42 cents per subscriber, compared to the 14 cents that BET was receiving. Likewise, the average 30-second ad on BET was selling for $1,500, compared to $3,500 for a 30-second ad on MTV.

Still, despite the disparity in revenue, BET's relative success had created a level of expectation that Johnson found impossible to meet. When he traveled to Hollywood, black producers and directors urged him to spend money to create original sitcoms and dramas. But to Johnson, the cost of producing original shows did not make economic sense for a network the size of BET. About 75 percent of the pilots produced on network television do not succeed, he pointed out. And then many of the other 25 percent of the successful shows are produced at a financial deficit because they will become profitable from the so-called "back end," when the repeat episodes are sold into syndication. "If we spend millions to produce original sitcoms, where are we going to back-end them?" Johnson would ask rhetorically. "There is not a huge secondary market for black programming. Who are we going to sell them to?"[13] Johnson was speaking from recent experience. In 1998, he purchased Arabesque Books, a line of African-American romance novels, from Kensington Publishing. Along with the list of 200 titles that the company held, the deal also called for BET to receive the dramatic rights to the books, which could be adapted for film and television.

BET used the titles to launch BET Pictures II, a film company aimed at producing 10 original movies in one year, at a cost of $1 million each. Black writers, directors, and actors in Hollywood "were thrilled," recalls Debra Lee. "We had events where they would come up to Bob and me and say 'Oh, thank you for this great opportunity. I don't ever get a chance to work. This is the greatest thing you guys have ever done.' "

This proved, however, to be a short-lived romance. BET's business model showed that in order for the movies to be profitable, each one had to air about 13 times during the year. By the time a film got to its fourth or fifth airing, however, viewers had grown sick of seeing it, and the ratings would plummet. Programming staffers came to Johnson and Lee, begging, "We've got to stop running these things so much."

BET executives then tried to offset the cost of making the films by selling the rights for foreign distributors to show the movies in other countries. They soon learned that there was no secondary market for their product, as the films attracted little attention from distributors. So, after making a total of 13 Arabesque films, BET backed off from the commitment. For far less money, the network could just show old black films from the 1970s and 1980s. "We found that we could acquire movies for cheaper than a million dollars and get a better rating," says Johnson.

Johnson also tried the same approach with situation comedies, making BET a back-end buyer for former broadcast network shows like 227 with Marla Gibbs and *Amen* with Sherman Hemsley, both of which originally aired on NBC. With the exception of a couple of original in-house productions such as *Blackberry Inn*, a cheesy situation comedy full of midgets, miniskirts, and missed attempts at humor, BET's sitcom lineup remained limited to the reruns of shows that had previously run on the major networks.

Yet Johnson became frustrated when he learned that the same shows that were once critically acclaimed and well received on network television were dismissed as junk once BET picked them up. "People loved these shows when they were on the networks," Johnson says. While another cable channel, Nickelodeon/Nick at Nite, was flourishing with nothing but repeats of old comedies, BET garnered criticism for running the hackneyed material. Nickelodeon, Johnson lamented, "has a whole network of these old shows. When they're on the white networks they're called classics. When they're on BET, they're called 'tired ol' reruns.'"

The critics came and went. And through it all, Johnson was fearless. He never backed down from a discussion and was always willing to listen—even if he hardly ever swayed from his course. Says former *Emerge* editor George Curry: "Bob is courageous, not afraid of controversy, and not afraid of taking a stand."

In fact, Johnson almost seemed to thrive on controversy. He and his network stirred passion in people, and that was good. Many people may have had nasty things to say about BET, but the important thing was that they were talking about the network. Most of the critics, he would contend, were people who did not understand his business. "Where do these people come from that they think they can sit back and criticize BET rather than going out and doing their own damn thing?" Johnson asked. "It's much easier to criticize. Much easier."[14]

There was, however, one BET critic who truly got under Johnson's skin. In 1999, Universal Press Syndicate had just launched a newspaper comic strip called "The Boondocks." Written by Aaron McGruder, a 25-year-old University of Maryland graduate, the strip focused on two young brothers who are black, and their experiences after moving from the South Side of Chicago to the all-white suburbs. It was funny, fresh, and irreverent, and McGruder infused each strip with a substantive and biting social and political subtext. He fired piercing arrows at people, pop culture, and institutions. From affirmative action opponent Ward Connerly to Sean "P-Diddy" Combs, *Star Wars*, and Santa Claus, McGruder named names and spared no one.

Although about 180 newspapers were carrying the strip, it was new and not many people had taken notice of it. But then, in late 1999, McGruder decided to use the strip to weigh in on BET. His first strip criticized the large number of bland infomercials on the network. In it, the main character, an afro-wearing child radical named Huey Freeman, calls his cable company to complain: "There seems to be a problem with my cable," Huey says to the person on the phone. "I'm watching Black Entertainment Television. But I don't see anyone black and it's not entertaining."

Soon after, in another strip, the character Huey is shown walking along and talking to a friend:

"I used to be a firm believer in the economic philosophy of Black Nationalism," Huey tells his friend.

"What's that?" the friend asks.

"That's the belief that black people have a responsibility to support all black businesses, because that creates a strong black economic base, powerful black entrepreneurs, etc. Those powerful black businesspeople would then act in the best interest of Black America."

"You don't believe in that anymore?" the friend asks.

Huey replies: "Let's just say BET shot a few holes in that theory."

McGruder was just getting started. He did more strips on BET, and then Johnson decided he had had enough. Other BET critics could be dismissed as people who were outside of BET's targeted demographic and therefore just didn't get it. But McGruder, a black man in his twenties, represented and spoke to BET's target audience, and he had a large forum, seven days a week. He was poised to become to the hip-hop generation what "Doonesbury's" Garry Trudeau was to baby boomers. Johnson found it difficult to just ignore McGruder. Plus, the comic strips were annoying the hell out of him.

The BET chief became so irate at "The Boondocks" that he started his own campaign to discredit the young cartoonist. He ran a letter in *Emerge* magazine and a letter in the *Washington Post* in which he responded to McGruder's strips and accused the cartoonist of sour grapes because he had once talked to BET about a possible television show based on the strip, and the network rejected the idea.

As Johnson's letter clearly showed, he was angry: "The most appalling of McGruder's reckless charges was that BET 'does not serve the interest of black people.' Our response to this slanderous assertion is that the 500-plus dedicated employees of BET do more in one day to serve the interest of African-Americans than this young man has done in his entire life."

Johnson's response was the best thing that could have happened to McGruder. "When he made an issue out of it," McGruder says, "it became an issue that black America became aware of, and in that process, black America became aware of me."

At that point, McGruder says, "I decided the gloves were off. I was going to go all out. It's not like there was a shortage of material there. It's not like I couldn't figure out a joke. There were plenty of jokes, and I had plenty of time."

Over the next couple of years, about 25 of "The Boondocks" strips would discuss BET. And soon, nearly every article that was written about BET would mention McGruder as one of the network's chief critics. Consequently, more and more people took notice of "The Boondocks." One strip on BET was even banned from some newspapers because it showed a salacious close-up of a woman's gyrating rear end, mocking what viewers see on BET's videos. The ban might have soothed Johnson's ire a slight bit, but it only stoked interest in "The Boondocks." Newspaper articles were written discussing the ban. "Everybody wanted to know why it was banned," says McGruder. "It was like a snowball effect."

McGruder never met Johnson, but he became one of Johnson's greatest nemeses. BET host Tavis Smiley, himself a critic of his employer's programming, tried a couple of times to get McGruder on his show, but the move was vetoed by someone upstairs in BET's executive offices. Then, when a compilation of McGruder's strips was published in book form in 2000, Johnson's wounds were reopened and salted and the relationship between him and Smiley was further damaged. The book, titled *The Boon-docks*, displayed a quote by Smiley on its cover: "McGruder is one of the most important voices of his generation and a true credit to his race," Smiley proclaimed. Inside the book, in his author's notes, McGruder added fuel to the fire by thanking Johnson for his success. McGruder laughs, "I know I must have driven him absolutely insane."

Johnson, for his part, continued to dismiss McGruder. "I read about this kid, this 'Boondocks' guy," Johnson said, his voice dripping with venom. "[How does] this guy think he has any kind of credibility to sit up and criticize BET?"[15]

Nevertheless, thanks in large part to Johnson and BET, by 2003 "The Boondocks" was running each day in over 260 newspapers, seen by more than 20 million people. Along with director Reggie Hudlin, McGruder was developing television and film projects for Sony Entertainment. The cartoonist was relishing the irony of his position:

"I've done a lot of things that have sparked controversy and discussion," McGruder said. "But BET was on a completely different level. I mean, it was the thing that people talked about when they talked about my strip. It's tough to work in the print medium and create relevance for yourself among young black Americans. And that's what the BET stuff did. That's exactly what it did. Bob tried to play Goliath. Which made me look like David. And who wins in that story?

"He can't carry this battle on for as long as I can," added McGruder. "He's got all the money in the world, but he can't carry on this battle like I can. And that's the irony of it. He's got a billion dollars, but in my little piece of real estate, I'm king. And all that money can't stop it. What's he going to do, write a letter to the editor every single day?"[16]

As each day faded to black, people closest to Johnson could see that he was growing exasperated by the criticism that his network was garnering. As Sheila Johnson recalls, "I could look in his face sometimes and see the hurt." Johnson became frustrated by his inability to quiet the critics. "It's like you can't win," he said. "No good deed goes unpunished."[17]

Still, he never let the frustration allow him to waver or lose sight of his main objective—earning a profit. "This was where Bob was exceptional," adds Sheila. "He stayed focused and went on."

WEALTH AND POWER

By the time he reached his 50th birthday in 1996, Bob Johnson was truly living the good life. He decided to commemorate the occasion by leasing a yacht, complete with a full crew, and inviting a dozen friends to join Sheila and him for a 10-day Mediterranean cruise.

As the huge, luxurious vessel sailed along the coast of Italy, Johnson and his friends sat up late into the night, sipping Dom Perignon, gossiping, joking, and relishing their station in life. During the day, when the boat pulled into ports, everyone stood on the deck, dressed in the finest white linens and nautical attire, giggling among themselves as the locals on the dock looked on in disbelief. "It was the most incredible experience," recalls Tim Reid, who was among the guests. "The sight of all these well-dressed black people pulling into port holding champagne glasses is one that I'll never forget."

Although he had always been relatively prudent about spending, Johnson was now beginning to invest heavily in his business as well as his personal life. Since going public a few years earlier, BET had been holding onto high amounts of cash and moving slowly to reinvest the money in the company. At the same time, Bob and Sheila—although they had already built a $2.5 million home with a tennis court and swimming pool in the "Gold Coast" section of northwest Washington and had purchased a new but modest house for Bob's mother in Freeport—had also been frugal with their newfound personal riches.

But in the mid-1990s, that all seemed to change, as the purse strings loosened. Over a period of a few years beginning around 1995, BET Holdings launched a string of joint ventures and partnerships, and ambitiously began extending the BET brand to everything from restaurants to clothing, books, credit cards, and magazines. In 1996, BET spent about $20 million reinvesting in the company. "How do you keep a business growing if you don't put money into it?" Johnson said at the time.[1]

And as his lavish birthday party indicated, the company's founder was also pumping up his personal lifestyle. That same year, he and Sheila plopped down $4.3 million to purchase a 168-acre estate in the lush and wealthy hunt country of Virginia. Located about an hour outside of Washington in the town of Middleburg, the vast expanse of green rolling hills and gated pastures, with a huge stone mansion and a barn for horses that would put most people's homes to shame, was named Salamander Farm.

The estate was a huge status symbol, as the Johnsons now lived in an area peopled by rich industrialists such as the Mellons and the DuPonts. Their nearby neighbors included Jackie Mars, of the candy bar fortune, and Abe Pollin, owner of professional basketball and hockey teams. The Johnsons' new role as members of the landed gentry took a little getting used to for some people in horse country. One morning when Johnson walked into the barn he encountered a white plumber who was there doing some work. "Excuse me," the plumber said to Johnson. "If you're down here to mop the arena, you know, you better hurry up because I'm getting ready to shut off the water."[2] The hapless plumber didn't realize that he was talking to the owner of the farm.

For Bob and Sheila, the purchase of Salamander Farm was also a major commitment to their daughter Paige, who at the age of 11 was deeply immersed in the world of show horses and equestrian competition. She was training a couple of hours each day and was already winning junior division events.

Bob and Sheila had been nurturing their daughter's love of horses for several years. On the morning of her sixth birthday, in 1991, they put Paige in the car—still dressed in her pajamas—and drove her to a stable in Maryland, where they surprised her with a new pony named Sailor.[3]

A pony was one thing, but becoming a serious equestrian was another. It is one of the most expensive and elite sports in existence, and one that few African-Americans have ever been exposed to as riders and competitors. People in the horse world were a little standoffish when Paige first started riding, but it did not take the Johnsons long to realize that the best way to gain acceptance in this rarefied new environment was to open their checkbook. They donated as much as $400,000[4] to help sponsor equestrian events, the tony festivals around the country where young heirs to some of the nation's greatest fortunes gather to face off in jumping competitions.

The Johnsons then startled many in the horse community when they began to purchase a string of expensive horses—or "mounts," as they are known—for Paige to ride in competition. Some of the horses cost them as much as $250,000 each, and the Johnsons' barn was eventually populated with more than a dozen of the pricey animals. "If you have to do it," Bob Johnson told *Spur* magazine, "you might as well do it in style."[5]

The couple's son, Brett, four years younger than Paige, took little interest in his sister's expensive hobby. Bob and Sheila bought Brett a pony also, but he was not inspired. Instead, he took to using the vast farmland to ride around on dirt-style motorbikes. As for the cost of the horses, Brett would quip: "There's a Lamborghini in every stall!"[6]

But Paige's talent for riding was prodigious. As she racked up one championship after another her name began gaining mention as a potential Olympic competitor. With this, the Johnsons upped the ante even more, purchasing Salamander South, a multimillion-dollar riding facility in Wellington, Florida, an equestrian community located 15 miles west of Palm Beach. Wellington is where the wealthiest of the riders train during the winter, and the 32-square-mile village includes homes owned by Cablevision founder Chuck Dolan and Netscape co-founder Jim Clark.

The Johnsons' entire Salamander Farm horse operation grew to employ a full-time staff of 20 people to care for the animals and stables and to train Paige. The high-security barns were equipped with video cameras aimed at the horses around the clock, and each groom received specialized training to drive the huge trucks that transported the horses. The entire annual operating expense rose to $6 million a year—all for Paige's horse fancy. "Every day I'm going to try to become a better rider, a better competitor," Paige said just before her 17th birthday. "I'll see where that takes me, where that leads me."[7]

So that they could still maintain a presence in Washington and be close to the business, the Johnsons also kept their home in the city. And around the same time that they bought Salamander Farm, BET Holdings was also moving into a brand-new six-story corporate headquarters that cost about $10 million to build. Located next to the production facility that BET had built six years earlier in the scuffed northeast section of the city, the sterling smoked-glass building was adorned on top with a huge gold star and black letters spelling "BET." Facing the railroad yard that connects Washington to cities along the northeast corridor, the building made a statement to all who took the train into the nation's capital. Washington was indeed the seat of the nation's power, but it was also home to a predominantly black population. BET's beautiful new headquarters sitting at the gateway provided an appropriate and poignant welcome to a place long known as "Chocolate City."

After having grown up alongside the railroad tracks in

Freeport, Illinois—a town like so many in the United States where blacks and whites, and haves and have-nots were divided by train tracks—Johnson was hypersensitive about the location of his new headquarters. When *Fortune* magazine in 1998 described the building as "hard by the railroad tracks" he took offense and telephoned the magazine, berating the writer for using such a description. "Bob called the writer and bitched at him for an hour," recalls a former BET executive. "And it was a positive story."

To complete the corporate campus, BET also constructed a new $8 million film and production facility adjacent to the new headquarters. Studio 2, as the facility was named, replaced the former production studio, which was turned into an operations and engineering center housing mostly technical equipment.

Studio 2 spoke volumes of Johnson's desire to establish the BET brand in motion pictures. He had already partnered in United Image Entertainment (UIE), a joint venture with Tim Reid (Butch Lewis also later invested in the venture). UIE was formed to develop and produce movies, and BET invested $1 million in the venture. To further fund the films and to secure distribution on pay television and in theaters, Johnson formed additional partnerships. One of these partnerships was BET Pictures, a joint venture with Blockbuster, and the other was BET Film Productions, a joint venture with Encore and Live Entertainment.

The 58,000-square-foot Studio 2, billed as state-of-the-art, was supposed to turn BET into a full-fledged Hollywood-style operation, with sound stages that could be leased out for major films and other independent productions. Initially, a few independent filmmakers tried using the studio. But while they loved the acoustics, they loathed the low ceilings and concrete floors that made it hard to build on. "It's an albatross," proclaimed Reid. Still, the studio provided a good home to many of BET's own productions.

To develop the films for the UIE partnership, Johnson and Reid called on established black directors, producers, and actors. Johnson and Reid thought that the idea of working for a black-owned studio would appeal to the Hollywood stars. But what they found was that people were skeptical of BET. Many of these big-name talents already had deals at the major studios, and they were not willing to commit to a fledgling operation like the one that Johnson and Reid were pitching. "There were a lot of skeptics," recalls Reid. "The respect aspect for BET was not too high. We couldn't get people, and that frustrated Bob, and frustrated me also."

UIE did manage to make four films, but it wasn't easy. It took more than six years to finance, cast, and produce the partnership's one major theatrical release, *Once Upon a Time . . . When We Were Colored*. The 1995 film had been budgeted at $4 million, but the partnership was able to raise just $2.5 million, so the production costs were trimmed. Based on a book by Clifton Taulbert about life in segregated Mississippi during the 1940s, the movie was directed by Reid and starred Al Freeman Jr., Phylicia Rashad, and Leon. It received favorable reviews from the critics, but ultimately grossed just $3.3 million at the U.S. box office. And as with all box office gross receipts, half of that money went to the movie theater operators, leaving the partners without enough to immediately recoup their investment and with a film that had little appeal in foreign markets.

Reid, who had spent much of his career acting in light-hearted comedies, knew that Hollywood did not show interest in many television shows or films that accurately and honestly depicted black life. For Reid, the partnership with BET offered an opportunity to tell black people's stories and build a library of major films that would be high in production value. Although Johnson shared some of those sentiments, his first priority, as always, was profits. He wanted to make movies, but did not want to risk very much of BET's capital to do so. At the same time, the more outside investors that they involved in a project, the more cumbersome it became. With the two men at odds over how to go about making movies, the partnership dissolved.

"He was going in one direction," says Reid. "I was going in another. I think he could have had both profits and good content. But that wasn't his interest. He has no interest in content and he used my own energy in that area." BET ended up with an ownership stake in the UIE films, yet Reid says he personally "never made a dime" from the venture. "I just hoped I would have gotten more out of it financially, and more respect," he laments.

A year or so later, Reid began raising money to launch his own studio and went to Johnson to ask if he'd be interested in investing. "No thanks," Johnson told his friend and former partner. "I've tried building a studio before and it did not work out." Nevertheless, in 1997 Reid hosted a grand opening for New Millennium Studios, a 52-acre facility, complete with back lot scenes of urban streets and the White House, located in St. Petersburg, Virginia. Johnson and his pal Butch Lewis traveled to St. Petersburg for the occasion. As they looked around at the place, Johnson was poker-faced, barely uttering a word. Reid, of course, was anxious to hear what Johnson thought of the place. Finally, after the tour was complete, Johnson approached Reid, looked him square in the eyes, and deadpanned: "You'll be out of business in six months." The two men burst out laughing.

Fortunately for Reid, Johnson's prediction was not accurate. New Millennium struggled for a while, but survived. After making a few films and other productions, Reid got a bit of poetic revenge. His company was chosen to become the main supplier for programming for TV One, an upstart cable channel aimed at competing with BET.

While Reid and Johnson parted ways, the bond between Johnson and Lewis grew stronger—professionally and personally. The two men had first teamed up together in 1991 to coproduce a three-hour pay-per-view special featuring the soul legend James Brown. The tribute to the man known as the God-father of Soul followed his release from prison, where he had served two years for assault, weapons charges, and eluding po-lice. The pay-per-view special was produced at a cost of about $3 million, but even after splitting the financial liability with Lewis and Time Warner, BET barely broke even.

Still, the business relationship between Lewis and Johnson was further cemented in 1999, when the American Federation of Television and Radio Artists (AFTRA) targeted BET for paying low wages to the comedians on *ComicView*. In a move that would help placate the unions, Butch Lewis Productions became pro-ducer of the show and reached an agreement with AFTRA, al-lowing for union members to receive a minimum pay scale, health and retirement benefits, residual fees, and travel ex-penses. It was hailed as the union's first pact with BET. But the deal was actually with Lewis' company, which allowed BET itself to avoid being locked into any collective bargaining agreement on other shows.

At least one other show, a sassy female talk fest called *Oh Drama!*, was also produced by Lewis, but it was clear to everyone involved with the shows that all of the work on the Butch Lewis productions was actually handled by BET employees. Phillip Johnson, former vice president of network operations at BET in Los Angeles, would fly into New York twice a month and spend the day at Lewis' office, handling all of the business and account-ing related to the two shows. "I functioned as Butch Lewis Pro-ductions," says Johnson, who was later fired from BET in a shake-up of the entertainment department. The arrangement continued years later. BET would get the programming without committing the entire network to a labor pact, and Lewis would collect a production fee.

In 1999, BET's chief financial officer, Dwight Crawford, says that he told Johnson that he believed the arrangement with Lewis was improper. Crawford was fired shortly thereafter, but in a lawsuit that he later filed against BET, he described the arrangement with Lewis:

> With the intent of evading liability for withholding of taxes from the wages of these employees, and in order to prevent a direct employer-employee relationship between BET and union members, BET arranged for Butch Lewis, a close personal friend of Mr. Johnson, to create a company called Butch Lewis Productions. BET and Mr. Lewis agreed that Butch Lewis Productions would pay wages to the production staff and provide them to BET, purportedly as independent contractors. BET would then pay Butch Lewis Productions a fee for the services of these workers. BET conducted all pre-hiring interviews of the production staff, made all decisions about selecting and hiring them, and instructed Butch Lewis Productions as to whom to place on its payroll. BET, and not Butch Lewis Productions, controlled and directed these workers in the performance of their duties, which were both necessary and incident to BET's business, and which were performed on BET's premises. Even though BET classified the production staff who were paid by Butch Lewis Productions as independent contractors, BET's relationship with these workers was actually one of employer and employee.[8]

Johnson dismissed Crawford's charges as the irrational rants of a disgruntled former employer. BET tried to have the case dismissed, saying it was without merit. A Washington superior court judge, however, ruled that the case should continue, and as of late 2003 it was still awaiting trial. The lawsuit also alleged that BET undertook other measures to avoid taxes.

Clearly, Johnson's relationship with Lewis was one of deep trust. Their arrangement helped Johnson solve his union problem, yet it also provided a nice situation for Lewis, who had always known how to hustle up a buck. A talkative, fun-loving, and likable man, Ronald "Butch" Lewis had been honing his business savvy since his early days in Philadelphia. His father owned a

used-car business, where Lewis himself worked. But he also sharp-
ened his business and negotiating skills on the city's streets. In a
1983 interview with the *New York Times*, Lewis described one of his
first business ventures:

> When I came out of high school I lived by my wits. In one in-
> stance, I had a friend of mine who worked in a jewelry store on
> Market Street. And I would gather maybe 20 rings—buy 'em in
> volume for a buck and a quarter apiece—and I'd be out on Market
> Street telling people these rings were worth $300, $400, $500, and
> all I wanted was $50. I'd say, "Look, you want to appraise it? Go
> ahead. Take it and have it appraised." The guy would go into the
> jewelry store, where my man was, right? My man puts the eyeglass
> on and looks at the ring, then says it's worth $1,500. The other
> guy comes hurrying out of the store, and he's happy to give me
> $50 for a ring that's worth $1.25.[9]

Lewis was introduced to boxing through his father, who was
among the local businesspeople who had invested in a promising
young Philadelphia fighter known as "Smokin' Joe" Frazier. As
Frazier rose to become the heavyweight champion of the world,
Lewis became a promoter of fights, styling himself in the outra-
geous and flamboyant fashion of Don King, who was already a
prominent figure on the fight scene. Just as King was known for
his high-top "crown" of a hairdo, Lewis became known for wearing a tuxedo with a bow tie around his neck, but no shirt on his
bare chest.

As an employee of Top Rank Inc., the firm owned by
Muhammad Ali's former promoter, Bob Arum, Lewis signed Leon
Spinks and Michael Spinks, two Olympic gold-medal winners
who had been brought up in the rugged ghetto of St. Louis.
Leon shocked the boxing world in 1978 when he snatched the
heavyweight crown from Ali. Soon thereafter, Lewis bolted from

Top Rank and struck out on his own as a promoter, taking Michael Spinks with him.

The big break for Lewis came in 1985 when Michael Spinks—a light heavyweight in physical stature—captured the International Boxing Federation's heavyweight title by defeating a much bigger Larry Holmes. That set up the big score: a 1988 fight against Mike Tyson, in which Spinks stayed on his feet for barely 60 seconds, but got up and walked away with a $13.5 million paycheck.

"I'm in the risk business," Lewis said. "You take a fighter and invest in him over a three-year period and you may never get your money back. But if you have the right heavyweight, you might make millions in one fight."

His fashion sense was unusual and he was rough around the edges, but people gravitated toward Lewis. Like the good promoter that he was, he was brash and loud, the very antithesis of Johnson. But Lewis appealed to Johnson and others as a streetwise trench-fighter—a short, scrappy guy who had the guts to compete in an unseemly business, facing off against intimidating types like the larger-than-life King. Lewis may have lacked sophistication, but he was a man of honor, a man's man. Besides, a person who can get ringside seats to championship fights has little problem making friends.

As he gained wealth and fame, Lewis became close friends with Johnson and with the film star Denzel Washington, who was emerging as one of the most prominent and highest-paid talents in Hollywood. The connection between the three men led to Denzel Washington joining the board of directors of BET Holdings. Clearly, Washington brought little business expertise to the board, but having the handsome Oscar-winning actor as a corporate director certainly added cachet to BET and offered a degree of validation to Johnson himself.

The high-rolling men would travel to professional fights together, attend entertainment industry events together, and party at each other's lavish homes. When Lewis celebrated his 50th birthday in June 1997, the guests who gathered at his Delaware estate included Joe Frazier; Michael Spinks; Denzel Washington and his wife, Pauletta; Tim Reid and his wife, the actress Daphne Maxwell Reid; and the singer James Brown. The Whispers and Bobby Womack entertained the guests. And Johnson, who also attended, paid to have an airplane deliver a birthday greeting to his friend, as a huge message reading "Big 50" flew over in the sky above the party.

Sheila Johnson and Pauletta Washington sometimes confided to each other that they could not understand why their husbands, who had such prominent, stellar public reputations, liked to pal around so much with a "rough dude" like Lewis. The wives would cringe with embarrassment when Lewis would show up at events they were hosting. (Sometimes he wore a shirt under his suit jacket, sometimes not.) "There is an allegiance to Butch," says Sheila Johnson, "that I just cannot quite understand."

Nevertheless, the men continued to hang tight through the years, and along with other well-known black men who were often a part of their group, they formed a unique coterie of power and fame. At the 2001 middleweight championship fight between Felix Trinidad and Bernard Hopkins, the Madison Square Garden crowd stirred loudly when Johnson, Washington, Lewis, and the actors Chris Tucker and Leon all walked in together, taking their seats near the ringside. It was a beautiful, rare sight: five black men who had achieved celebrity and fortune, just hanging out, chillin'. At that moment, Hollywood's once notorious Rat Pack seemed passé, like tired ancient history.

Such occasions offered a refuge for Johnson, a chance for him to be just another brother, out with his boys. His network of friends and associates had now grown to become vast and powerful. Just like early in his life, when he was able to thrive in all-white environments and ingratiate himself with all the right people, Johnson was now flourishing in elite, rarefied circles. He was invited to join the boards of major corporations, becoming a director at companies such as General Mills, US Airways, and Hilton Hotels. He even gained an invitation to the annual exclusive gathering of international media tycoons held in Sun Valley, Idaho, and hosted by the New York investment bank Allen & Company.

As a former Washington lobbyist and political operative, Johnson showed a huge appreciation for the importance of cultivating friends in high elected offices. As his personal wealth grew, he gave generously to political parties and individual campaigns, and he eventually even made a donation of $1 million to the Democratic National Committee. He and Sheila hosted President Bill Clinton at Democratic fund-raisers held at their Washington home, and they, too, were guests at the White House for state dinners.

Johnson had learned the value of access and influence early on. Shortly after launching BET, he had worked the local corridors of power in Washington, D.C., supporting the city's popular mayor, Marion Barry. It apparently paid off. In 1984, Johnson put together a group of dozens of local investors to bid for the franchise rights to install and operate the city's cable system. The group was led by Johnson, and included his business partner, the venture fund head Herb Wilkins, and another close friend and former Federal Communications Commissioner, Tyrone Brown. The lead investors, including Johnson, put up $150,000 each, and Wilkins' venture fund, Syncom, invested $300,000.

But the real linchpin in the deal was John Malone's TCI. The D.C. city council, which Barry lorded over, wanted to award the franchise to a minority-owned firm, so TCI stood no chance of winning the rights on its own. Instead, Malone agreed to partner with Johnson's group, District Cablevision Inc., taking 49 percent of the equity and providing the financing to build the $130 million system. Johnson's group did indeed win the franchise, but soon thereafter began complaining that it could not adequately fund the project without more help from TCI. As a result, the controlling equity in District Cablevision was sold to TCI. So much for the city council's desire to place the potentially lucrative franchise in the hands of a minority-owned business—a nonminority firm ended up with the cable franchise after all. It was a turn of events that only fueled criticism by those who had been asserting all along that Johnson was Malone's "front man."

But there were no tears shed by Johnson and his partners. According to Wilkins, by the time Johnson's partners sold the remainder of their equity in the late 1990s, each original $150,000 investment was worth about $2.5 million.

With his business headquartered in Washington, it was indeed wise for Johnson to have Barry as a friend. According to the *Washington Post*, Johnson allowed the mayor to use his Delaware beach house, and he counseled Barry following the mayor's 1990 arrest, when a police videotape of Barry smoking crack cocaine was aired nationwide.[10]

By the mid-1990s, however, Johnson had influence with many people who were far more powerful than the troubled, embattled mayor. And with his growing ambition, Johnson was sure to one day need President Clinton or other Democratic leaders.

In the meantime, Johnson immersed himself in all the fine things that his newfound wealth afforded him. He sent his children to the prestigious Sidwell Friends School that Chelsea Clinton and the kids of many other influential Washingtonians attended and where his wife had taught. He bought a vacation home in Anguilla. He even sponsored two young tennis players from the tiny Caribbean island, helping them attend college in the United States.

When Johnson wasn't working on his own tennis game in his backyard or relaxing at one of his homes, he sought out other activities, sometimes with his folks back in the Midwest. Using a private jet, he'd fly out to visit family members in Wisconsin and Freeport. There, he and his brothers would jump back on the plane and fly off to go squirrel hunting along the Mississippi River.

After the bad experience with his sister Paulette, he had not brought any family members other than his wife into the BET corporate suite. But each year, Johnson gave generous monetary gifts to each member of his huge family. They showed their appreciation, using the money for their own small business ventures, and guarding their now famous brother's privacy with a vengeance. "His immediate family is very protective of him," insisted Johnson's older sister, Joyce Boggess, owner of a child care business in Madison, Wisconsin. "We don't talk publicly about Bob."

Clearly, Johnson was proud of his ability to enrich his family. Speaking before a group of black newspaper columnists, he said, "When I got to the point that I could give $100,000 to each of my family members, I knew that money was no problem." He helped to support his stepmother even after his father, Archie, had died in 1995 at the age of 84. And when Johnson's own mother, Edna, died in 2001 at age 87, he gave $100,000 to endow a scholarship for African-American women in her honor at a local Freeport school, Highland Community College.

Now that his business was an undisputed success, Johnson set his sights on the ultimate rich guy's toy: a professional sports team. He had first tested the waters in 1991, when he briefly joined with a group that was seeking to bid for a National Football League expansion team in North Carolina.

But in 1994, Johnson made an all-out effort to build a stadium in Washington, D.C., and gain control of the Washington Bullets basketball team at the same time. Johnson evisioned combining the team with his cable channel the way that Ted Turner had combined the Atlanta Hawks and Atlanta Braves with Turner Broadcasting. What better place for a black cable channel to own a team than right in Washington, where the population was overwhelmingly black?

But Abe Pollin, the longtime owner of the Bullets as well as the professional hockey team, the Washington Capitals, was not interested in selling. Pollin was already negotiating to move the teams from their home in suburban Maryland to a new arena in downtown Washington. The plan called for a $200 million, 21,000-seat arena to be built, and Pollin was asking taxpayers to foot most of the bill.

Johnson upset Pollin's plans when he announced that BET would build the stadium using its own money. Johnson sought to gain the right to build the stadium, and in the process obtain control of Pollin's lease terms and ultimately gain control of the teams.

Johnson's move forced city leaders to reassess whether taxpayers should pay for the stadium. Johnson filed a lawsuit seeking to stop Pollin's deal and tried to appeal to city leaders and to Pollin on the grounds of race. In an interview with the *Washington Post*, Johnson recounted speaking with Pollin about the possibility of selling the team to BET. "So I made the appeal from a sociological perspective," Johnson said. "I told him, 'Abe, you're from the suburbs, I'm from the city. You're white. I'm black. The city is mostly black, and the players are too.' "[11]

Pollin did not go for it. Instead, he agreed to pay for the stadium himself. Pollin moved his teams into the new MCI Arena in 1997. Because Washington had been beset by so much gun violence, the basketball team's name was changed—the Bullets became the Wizards. Johnson's foray into professional sports would have to wait.

Owning the teams surely would have made the Mississippi native an official Washingtonian. Despite all of his connections and political involvement, Johnson always seemed to be yearning to be truly accepted, a man the hometown folks would be proud of. According to Sheila, "Bob has never felt as though he really has belonged. Washington was a hard town to live in. You just have a hard time fitting in."

In a city where most of the big shots are those who are voted into their jobs, and respect is accorded based on the intellectual prestige of one's work, Johnson was destined to be a bit of an outsider. This was a town, after all, where everyone professed—sincerely or not—to be working for some greater good. Bob Johnson did not espouse such pretentious notions of himself and his work. He was an iconoclast, a stubborn man living in a town that believed in institutions and thrived through the art of compromise.

Sometimes, Johnson seemed to relish being contrary and controversial. Even when he knew it would rile some observers, he would readily make it clear that his business interests were his primary concern, and he would not hesitate to cite hypocrisy in the industry. He accepted liquor ads on BET while most other channels ran scared of the criticism the ads might garner. He also fought Washington's attempts to force television networks to place violence ratings on their programs. "Now, this is bullshit," Johnson declared in *MediaWeek* in 1997. "Don't say to me 'you should be concerned about protecting poor black people, so do the ratings, keep off the liquor ads.' If you want to put me in charge of helping minorities, I can think of a hell of a lot more things that are more important than TV ratings and banning liquor ads."[12]

Later that year, on a December evening, Johnson arrived at his favorite after-work spot, the exclusive Four Seasons Hotel in Georgetown. He often retired to the posh hotel after a day at the office, sometimes for dinner with associates in the hotel's restaurant, and other times for a drink in the lounge with a friend. He had never forgotten the day when he was sitting in his Jaguar in front of the hotel and a white lady walked out, opened his rear door, and jumped into the backseat. She thought that Johnson was her chauffeur. He and his friends laughed for years about little "Miss Daisy."

There was no mistaking Bob Johnson on this particular evening at the Four Seasons. Dozens of black professionals were arriving at the hotel to join Johnson. Every now and then he would invite 50 to 100 people to gather for drinks and hors d'oeuvres, and then a guest speaker would address the group. As soon as Johnson arrived, he spotted Dwight Ellis, vice president of the National Association of Broadcasters, which represents the interests of the nation's local broadcasters in Washington. Ellis, a black man who had known Johnson for years, had recently been quoted in the *Washington Post*, strongly criticizing Johnson and the quality of programming on BET.

"How ya doin', Dwight?" Johnson asked, slapping his nemesis on the back. Ellis looked nervous. He wasn't sure how much his recent comments had angered Johnson.

"I read your comments," Johnson said. "You definitely don't understand business."

But Ellis did not back down. "You have held yourself up as representing the African-American community, and I resent it," he replied to Johnson. "And everybody here resents it." With that, all of the people who were standing around within earshot began to scatter like mice. But Ellis continued, as if he was finding comfort in purging himself of pent-up emotions. "There are some drug dealers making millions," Ellis said. "Should I respect them because they are millionaires? In my view," he told Johnson, "you're one of the most dangerous black men in America." With that, Johnson uncharacteristically gave up on the argument. "Ahhhh," he moaned with resignation. "I don't want to talk about it anymore." He walked away to schmooze with other guests.[13]

THE BLACK DISNEY

Like a budding teenager teeming with hormones and attitude, BET was growing up. And inside corporate headquarters during the mid-1990s, the evolution became more tangible with each passing day.

Gone were the days when employees could run into Johnson in the hallway and engage the boss in an impromptu chat. To enter the gated, campuslike facility, workers drove past a guard's booth to a sprawling outdoor parking lot. Johnson and his staff of senior executives, however, drove their cars through a separate gate, parked beneath the building, and used a special elevator key to access the corporate suite atop the building on the sixth floor. While the rank and file chowed down in the cafeteria on the first floor, Johnson and his lieutenants were dining on catered meals in the executive quarters upstairs. Any employee or visitor who did manage to reach the top floor stepped off the elevator to be greeted by a security guard. And when they did happen to see Johnson, or just speak to each other about him, he was no longer referred to as "Bob." Now he was known strictly as "Mr. Johnson."

Even the annual picnic, which for so long had been the one place where regular workers could count on rubbing elbows with the brass, was eliminated. In its place, the company started shutting down the cafeteria on Friday afternoons during the summer and serving barbecue outside under a large white canopy. On rare occasions, Johnson would even wander downstairs for barbecue. But the mood was more uptight at the workplace than it had been at a picnic. When employees spotted him, they would begin to eat faster, and then rush back to work. The summer barbecue was a sweet touch, but BET was no longer a small, homey shop. It was becoming a media giant.

Since the public offering, the number of employees had grown steadily, reaching nearly 500 nationwide by the mid-1990s. And a strict hierarchy ruled the corporate culture, as Johnson and his senior executives stayed away from the lower floors of the headquarters building as well as the adjacent studio and production facilities. Inside the suite, a "gentleman's gentleman" whom everyone knew as "Delmar" was always on standby to function as Johnson's lifeline to the daily public routines, handling trivial tasks like running to the drugstore, picking up clothes from the dry cleaners, or dropping the car off at the shop for service.

The chief executive's suite was sleek and contemporary, furnished with rich mahogany, black leather, and black-themed sculptures and paintings. Inside Johnson's crescent-shaped office, three huge television screens were recessed into the wall, positioned so he or his guests could see them either from his desk or from the sofa and seats at the other end of the room.

Top news anchors and other on-air talent could usually get an audience with Johnson, but mostly he stuck firmly to the chain of command, having his information and reports passed up through management to his senior executives. It was just the way a major corporation should work—when indeed it worked correctly. Sometimes the rigid separation led to communications breakdowns that made the company seem cold and impersonal. In 1997, when *Video Soul*, the music program that for years had been hosted by Donnie Simpson, was canceled, network executives began planning a big final show. But no one bothered to inform Simpson himself about his grand finale, until the day before the show was scheduled to be shot. "No one had told me about it," recalls Simpson, who was so annoyed by the slight that he chose not to take part in the final segment of the program that he had launched 14 years earlier. "I never got to say goodbye because of the way it ended."[1]

Only one executive vice president, Curtis Symonds, the sociable head of affiliate sales, regularly walked the hallways and ate lunch in the cafeteria. There, Symonds could often be found, laughing and freely mingling among the staff. Even Jeff Lee, the head of programming, started distancing himself from lower-ranking members of his staff. In BET's earlier days, Lee had spent lots of time hanging around the studio, making sure productions went well. Because of his close relationship with Johnson, Lee was viewed by his staff as the one executive they could count on to appeal to Johnson to provide resources for shows. "Bob, we can't do this shit without more money," Lee would tell the boss. Sometimes Lee even prevailed, convincing Johnson to commit a few more bucks for a new set or a production assistant.

But Lee was now firmly positioned to one day succeed Johnson. Consequently, he also hunkered down in the corporate suite and became less accessible.

But on March 19, 1996, Johnson stunned Jeff Lee and the rest of the company when he and his board of directors named Debra Lee, the general counsel and head of business development, to serve as the company's president and chief operating officer. The newly created position made Debra Lee the company's undisputed second-in-command and Johnson's likely successor. Johnson openly gushed over his newly appointed, demure, Ivy League–educated president. "I don't think there's a black woman in the country who's higher ranking in authority than Debra Lee," he proudly proclaimed.[2]

With his decision to select Debra Lee over Jeff Lee, Johnson bypassed his longtime confidant and friend. And while it was a victory for black women in corporate America, it was a devastating blow to Jeff Lee, and his disappointment was palpable to everyone around him. He continued in his job, but his responsibilities were slowly and steadily diminished.

Meanwhile, the business was booming. In 1996, BET's revenue reached a record high of $133 million, a 15 percent increase over the previous year. The company's earnings before interest, taxes, depreciation, and amortization (EBITDA)—the measure that the media industry commonly uses as an indicator of a firm's ability to fund its operations—increased by 13 percent, to $49.9 million. Net income was $22 million, an 11 percent increase from the previous year. Continuing to add subscribers at a rate of 3 to 4 million per year, the network was now reaching 45.2 million households, or slightly more than half the country's homes that received cable television.

In the relatively short period of 16 years, the company had come a long way from its humble start. Major media outlets were taking notice and heaping praise on the company. *BusinessWeek*, in its annual "Hot Growth Companies" issue, selected BET as one of the 100 Best Small Corporations. And *Forbes* magazine placed BET on its yearly list of the 200 best small companies in the United States. By 1997, the company had undergone such a long period of sustained revenue growth and expansion that *Black Enterprise* magazine named it the "1997 Company of the Year."

Johnson was now demonstrating to Wall Street and to the world that he wanted BET to be much more than a cable channel. His company had gained broad recognition among the country's 30 million black Americans, a segment of the population that had estimated annual spending power of $500 billion yet was vastly underserved in the marketplace. Why couldn't BET reach beyond its core cable television product and serve that market with other goods and services? As Johnson saw it, there was no reason that BET couldn't do just that. He had accumulated a talented management team. The channel was generating huge amounts of cash, so there was capital to spend on new ventures. And more importantly, the company had a brand that it could build upon.

BET started investing its capital in a wide range of new businesses, usually partnering with mainstream firms that had a desire to reach black consumers. In fact, Johnson was a master at forming partnerships, which he believed were the best way to grow the business. That way, BET shared the risk and gained access to additional funding and expertise. And by affiliating with BET, other firms could gain access to the black marketplace. "The smartest way for an African-American company to grow is by strategic partnerships," Johnson said. "We don't have to have 100 percent black ownership."

But creating successful new businesses would not be easy, Johnson would learn. His tough experiences with expansion efforts made his main cable network seem like a fortuitous gold strike.

One of BET's earliest expansions was its 1993 purchase of 80 percent of Action Pay-Per-View. BET paid an estimated $10 million to purchase the movie channel—which had five million subscribers—from Avalon Communications. BET changed the format to feature mostly black-themed films. But with it still losing about a half million dollars per year, BET Action Pay-Per-View eventually started showing original adult programs. One of the channel's most popular features was *Luke's Peep Show*, in which subscribers paid $8 to $10 per view to watch the hip-hop star Luther Campbell frolick with naked women. Additionally, the company entered a joint venture with Encore Media Corporation, launching BET Movies/Starz!, a 24-hour premium movie channel.

Johnson also invested in restaurants, first opening BET SoundStage, an entertainment-themed restaurant in Largo, Maryland, amid the wealthy black suburbs of Washington. On its opening night, superstars like Aretha Franklin and Boyz II Men joined Johnson to toast the new business, which featured

42 monitors that played music videos and a dining room that gave customers the feeling of being in the middle of a video production. Even though it had an inauspicious start (in its first year of business in 1997, BET SoundStage had revenues of $3.4 million but lost about $1 million), the company had plans to open 20 more of the restaurants around the country. A waterfront SoundStage nightclub was opened at Disney World's Pleasure Island in Florida in a partnership with the Walt Disney Company, which was working hard at the time to attract black visitors to its amusement parks.

Only two more restaurants were ever opened. BET on Jazz Supper Club, a pricey, upscale place with haute cuisine and live jazz, was located in downtown Washington. But alas, with this venture BET's executives learned that their valuable brand could also be poison. Despite a prime location on 11th Street, right among the city's white politicians, lawyers, lobbyists, and sight-seers, the Washington restaurant attracted only black diners, not sufficient enough numbers to justify its expensive location. "Because we had black as part of the name, we got all black customers," recalls Gloria Nauden, who worked as BET's creative director for the restaurants. "We did not attract what downtown D.C. is really about."

Leveraging Johnson's position as a member of the board of Hilton Hotels, BET even explored a grand plan to build a $250 million SoundStage hotel and casino in Las Vegas. The two companies decided not to pursue the plan, but they did later partner to open another jazz-themed restaurant. But this one, located inside Hilton's Paris Hotel and Casino in Las Vegas, did not bear the BET name. Instead, it was named Très Jazz, with no hint of a connection to a black-owned firm. "We couldn't put the BET brand on it because we were in white Vegas," said Nauden. "It would have been suicidal."

Nevertheless, over several years the BET brand was emblazoned on a wide range of products and services.

In an attempt to sell merchandise directly to viewers, Johnson launched BET Direct, selling clothing, music, and jewelry. Partnering with Home Shopping Network, *BET Shop*, a three-hour shopping program, began airing. BET even attempted to break into the ethnic beauty products business with an exclusive line of products called "Color Code." The skin creams, facial masks, and lotions were sold during the annoying half-hour infomercials that played late at night on the network.

Through a joint venture with G-III Apparel Group, a line of casual clothing, aimed at buyers between the ages of 16 and 30, was initiated. And in conjunction with Chevy Chase Bank, BET Financial Services was launched. The first planned product was a co-branded Visa credit card. Neither the clothing line nor the financial services firm ever made a profit before they were scrapped.

In fact, there were plenty of short-lived ventures. The company invested $5 million in Urban City Foods, a firm that was developing Burger King restaurants in African-American communities around the country. A black fast-food entrepreneur, La-Van Hawkins, who had first struck it big developing Checkers hamburger franchises, controlled Urban City. BET promised to loan Urban City up to $10 million to help fund a plan to expand to a total of 225 Burger King restaurants. But Hawkins soon found himself entangled in a long and nasty court battle with the Burger King Corporation, and by the time it was all settled, Urban City was forced to forgo its expansion plans and Hawkins had to sever all ties with the burger company.

Additionally, BET invested $1 million in Cybersonic Records, a partnership that Johnson struck with Ernie Singleton, a music industry veteran who had had a long and distinguished career that included serving as the head of black music at MCA Records and as the chief executive of the highly successful rap label Ruthless Records. Singleton and

Johnson had faced off earlier when MCA sold exclusive rights to some of its videos to MTV, but the two men later joined together at Cybersonic, which was planning to release new pop, rhythm and blues, and hip-hop on a new label called Fully Loaded Records. To help get the company going, BET agreed to loan an additional $3 million, but the label never got off the ground and the partnership dissolved.

In dealing with his partners, Johnson was sometimes like a runaway bride, going right to the altar but then getting cold feet when it was time to commit major funding. He wanted to diversify, but he could not stomach the idea of disturbing the parent company's profit margins. A partnership would come apart, usually due to a lack of resources. The partner would often feel burned and sometimes lose money. Yet Johnson always seemed to have structured the partnership in a way that saved himself and his company from taking too much of a hit. As Tim Reid, one of Johnson's scorned partners, put it: "Bob always came out intact."

Johnson's reluctance to invest in his ancillary businesses sometimes belied his sound business judgment. In the late 1990s, when BET Action Pay-Per-View was on the verge of becoming the company's first profitable venture beyond the network, Johnson was offered a big break. Showtime Entertainment, which had a contract with the former heavyweight champion Mike Tyson, offered to give BET's pay-per-view channel the exclusive right to air the unpredictable fighter's next five bouts. With Tyson's infamy and ability to draw viewers, it was a sure way to quickly increase distribution and instantly validate BET as a major player in the pay-per-view business. There was one small catch. To gain the rights to the fights, BET had to pay $10 million in up-front fees, mostly to cover costs to the promoters.

Curtis Symonds, who was running BET's pay-per-view business at the time and had been negotiating for months with Showtime to get the fights, provided Johnson with estimates that showed BET earning several million on each fight, based on modest sales projections. "Bob, we can make $10 million just standing still," Symonds declared, unable to contain his excitement.

But as if the offer was too good to be true, the chief executive was reluctant to put the money up. "Bob, this is Mike Tyson," Symonds cried. "We can't pass this up." But Johnson needed to be convinced. In an attempt to sway him, Symonds invited Matt Blank, the head of Showtime's boxing business, to come down from New York for dinner in Washington. During the meal, Blank looked Johnson in the eyes and confirmed the offer. "I will give you Mike Tyson," Blank said.

But Johnson refused to do the deal. In response, Symonds went ballistic. "Bob, I can't bring you anything," he yelled. "Of all the businesses we've had, I'm so close to finally cracking a profit with this one. These fights would have gotten us over the hump." But Johnson was as calm as ever. "I just can't see fronting the $10 million," he explained to Symonds. The heads of other BET businesses were frustrated in similar ways, Symonds contends. "We in the trenches could see what we needed to do, but he wouldn't loosen the financial reins," Symonds said.

Sticking closer to what the company did best, Johnson in 1996 launched another cable channel, BET on Jazz. The 24-hour jazz music channel, which featured original studio performances, live festivals, and variety shows hosted by musicians, was an attempt to attract the older, more affluent viewers who had little interest in the rap and hip-hop that dominated the main network. The company also hoped that the worldwide popularity of jazz would help to build BET's fledgling international business, which had grown to include distribution in more than a dozen countries, including South Africa, Japan, and Canada. But the jazz channel struggled to attract viewers. After starting with one million subscribers, it added less than a million each year. After two years, the channel had total losses of nearly $10 million.

The magazine publishing business had its struggles also. Wall Street analysts complained about the $2 million per year in ongoing losses at the teen magazine *YSB*, forcing Johnson to finally shutter the title in 1996. Yet the following year, the company entered into a partnership with the *New York Daily News* to publish a newspaper insert, *BET Weekend*. Distributed inside daily and weekly newspapers around the country, the lifestyles and entertainment monthly had an instant audience, with its circulation reaching over one million in its first year. But in the case of an insert, there are no additional circulation revenues so all that really matters is advertising. And the ad sales were not as strong as the partners had anticipated. "The thing was a much harder sell than we had thought it would be," said one of the *Daily News* executives who managed the partnership.

Johnson never involved himself much in the magazine business, leaving it to his editors and publishers. "Bob did not meddle," recalls Yannick Rice Lamb, who was editor of *BET Weekend*. Still, however, he did relish the chance to use the magazines to create buzz and stir controversy. "Make the covers more provocative," he would suggest, according to George Curry, who was editor of BET's first and longest-running title, *Emerge*. When *Emerge* ran a cover illustration of Supreme Court Justice Clarence Thomas with a slavelike red-and-white bandanna tied around his head, it attracted nationwide attention and prompted a number of personal calls to Johnson from politicians and others who complained that the handkerchief head imagery was mean and over the top. "It's George's magazine," Johnson explained, feigning a studied indifference to the snarky cover. Privately, however, Johnson and Curry got together and laughed like crazy about the Thomas cover.

Despite the buzz that such issues generated, *Emerge* lost money each year, contributing largely to total operating losses of $3 million annually for the entire magazine unit.

Nevertheless, in a move to further expand the magazine publishing division and sell advertising across a broader platform of titles, BET paid about $4 million to purchase a women's health and fitness title, *Heart & Soul*, from Rodale Publishing. Johnson first learned about the magazine from its founder, Reginald Ware. Ware had sold 80 percent of the equity in *Heart & Soul* to Rodale in 1992 in exchange for a $5 million investment in the magazine. The four-year-old title was growing rapidly, with revenues increasing 150 percent each year. But then in 1995, Rodale and Ware became entangled in a legal dispute. A string of lawsuits and charges ensued, and during that time Rodale managed to seize Ware's equity stake.

A small entrepreneur who lacked the financial wherewithal to take on a publishing power like the Pennsylvania-based Rodale, Ware sought out Johnson. "I went to him for advice on what I should do," Ware recalls. "He said there was nothing I could do but fight it in court." But while the two men were talking, Ware filled Johnson in on the magazine's financial potential. "During our meeting, I told Bob what a profitable entity the magazine was. So he knew it was a gold mine." Indeed, in 1998, while Ware was still struggling to fight Rodale in court and hoping to reclaim *Heart & Soul*, Johnson purchased it from under his nose. "I got screwed out of the deal," says Ware, who went on to publish *T&E*, a multicultural travel and entertainment magazine. "The lawsuits put pressure on Rodale so they sold him the magazine. But I don't have any animosity toward Bob."

By the late 1990s, many people were referring to BET not as a cable company, but as a media empire. Even though some of his new ventures were off to shaky starts, Johnson remained confident of his vision—so much so that he was making the heady prediction that one day BET would be to black people what the entertainment giant the Walt Disney Company is to the mainstream consumer.

In April 1999, the CBS Sunday night newsmagazine *60 Minutes* did a feature story on Johnson. "You want to turn BET into a black Disney?" the show's host, Morley Safer, asked Johnson. "I would be proud to have BET's brand have the same clout that the Disney brand has," Johnson replied. (Johnson later grew to despise the 60 *Minutes* story. The segment took viewers inside his vast Salamander Farm and showed the world how fabulously wealthy he had become. Safer labeled him "the backwoodsman from Illinois as country squire." Some people who saw the 60 *Minutes* piece accused Johnson of stuffing his own pockets instead of reinvesting in improving the network. "A lot of black folks took it the wrong way," says one BET executive. And a former BET on-air host adds, "Bob goes on 60 *Minutes* and people see how rich he is and they no longer want to hear that 'We're a small black company' excuse anymore.")

By pursuing the entertainment and leisure dollars spent by black consumers, Johnson was indeed trying to mold his company into one similar to Disney. But even more than that, what Johnson was more specifically mimicking was the success of his business partner, John Malone. Malone's TCI had become so powerful, dominating such a large percentage of the country's cable systems, that virtually all cable programmers had to go through TCI to be successful. In a similar manner, Johnson was trying to turn BET into the gatekeeper for black America. And it was evident by all of the companies that struck partnerships with Johnson that many mainstream firms valued the access that BET had to black consumers.

But the people who were buying BET shares were not thrilled with all of the diversification. Fund managers on Wall Street complained that the new ventures did not complement the core cable product. It was the era of the media conglomerate, when major companies like Viacom, Disney, and Time Warner were acquiring various broadcast, cable, film, print, and Internet properties, all in the name of so-called synergy. All the pieces were supposed to work together and complement each other. Operating costs could be cut, marketing efforts combined, and advertising packaged and sold at one time for use across various mediums.

Johnson, too, was caught up in the zeitgeist of the moment. If the big boys could become conglomerates, then why couldn't he? The problem was that BET was not one of the big boys, and Johnson's moves into other businesses were not like the major acquisitions that the big companies were engaging in. Many of his new businesses were detached from each other. They were targeted at black people, but that was all that they had in common. The only synergistic connection was race.

Moreover, BET was starting new ventures from scratch, diversifying in an entrepreneurial manner. Wall Street investors liked BET as just a cable company, regularly generating fat profit margins of more than 40 percent. They did not like the idea that Johnson was now using those profits to start a wide assortment of new businesses that they felt had little synergy or added little value to the core cable product. These were the types of moves that investors felt should be funded with venture capital. What Johnson saw as new ideas for growing his company, Wall Street decried as a poor use of profits and an overambitious desire to build an empire.

The truth is few money managers on Wall Street really understood BET. They were mostly white men who had little interest in the network, and were not inclined to spend much time learning about the product or the market that it was trying to serve. They were comfortable with BET only if it stuck to its plain-chocolate core. One analyst in *Fortune* magazine called BET a "confusing story."[3] Johnson's diversification moves were dismissed as scattershot and ill-advised, and as a result the company's stock languished. While other media and entertainment companies were trading at multiples of about 20 times their earnings, BET stock traded in the lowly range of 10 to 12 times earnings.

Johnson began to insist that the company was misunderstood and undervalued. In an attempt to help investors better grasp his vision, he traveled to New York and met with dozens of analysts. But it did little to help, as the price of a share of BET remained stuck at around $30, just $5 or $6 above the price it closed at on the day of its IPO. The low stock price was preventing BET from using its shares to acquire or invest in other companies. As Johnson saw it, his desire to build a brand that could target the black consumer in many ways was being stymied only by a lack of vision on Wall Street. And his partner Malone agreed. Because of the depressed shares, Malone said, BET had no "invasion capital."[4]

But the two men were fully confident that based on the fast-growing value of the cable network alone, BET was worth much more than the price that the stock market was placing on it. And that spelled opportunity.

It was time, Johnson and Malone decided, to buy out the public shareholders and make the company their own private entity once again. But before they could pull it off, things would get very ugly inside BET.

COSTLY AFFAIRS

The 1997 BET executive retreat was much bigger than in previous years. Usually, Johnson and his six or seven executive vice presidents would escape the chilly Washington winter and jet off for the annual getaway, checking into resorts in warm weather places such as Florida and Arizona. As they huddled in their luxurious surroundings, the network honchos would discuss strategy for their individual operations and gather for a dinner at which Johnson would deliver a speech outlining the past year's performance, ongoing concerns, and future goals. His talk was referred to as "Bob's state of the union."

This year's speech promised to be special. For the first time, Johnson had invited all of his senior vice presidents and vice presidents, meaning that this year there would be about 40 people at the retreat, being held in Palm Beach, Florida. He had something he wanted them all to hear.

In the weeks leading up to the retreat, Johnson had begun trying to repurchase the 36 percent of BET that he and Malone's Liberty Media Corp. did not already own. Liberty was the cable-programming unit that Malone had spun off from his TCI cable systems and was also controlled by him. Johnson and Malone had offered $48 per share for the six million outstanding shares in BET, which meant that based on the offered price they would pay a total of $288 million to complete the proposed buyback. This valued the entire company at $800 million, not accounting for $60 million in outstanding debt.

Shareholders, however, were certain to demand a higher price before selling their stakes, so Johnson knew that he was about to take on a much larger debt load to buy his company back. With BET's strong cash flow, borrowing the money would not be difficult. But Johnson wanted to keep the overall price as low as possible, and to do so he had to deal with an additional financial issue. His six top executives had been accumulating stock options that were now worth a total of about $40 million. They, too, had to be bought out.

In an attempt to ease the total financial burden of regaining complete ownership of his company, Johnson made an audacious request. He asked the executives simply to hand over 50 percent of their options, which would shave about $20 million off the price of repurchasing the company. "Will we be owners in the new company?" Jeff Lee asked, dumbfounded by the suggestion that he and the others just give up what they had earned for helping to make BET a success.

To facilitate his attempted buyback and to continue with their brand expansion and broad diversification, Johnson asked that all of them, together, agree to forgo the options.

All six of the executives, except for the chief financial officer, William T. Gordon III, had been at the company since its fledgling years in the early 1980s. There was Debra Lee, the chief operating officer; Jeff Lee, the head of programming; Janis Thomas, who now ran marketing; Curtis Symonds, the head of affiliate sales; and the advertising sales chief, James Ebron. All of them felt a deep sense of loyalty not only to BET, but most of all to Johnson personally. "To some degree we looked at him as a dad, always wanting to please him," recalls one of the executives.

Gordon, however, who had joined the company just four years earlier in the wake of the embezzlement scandal that sent his predecessor Antonia Duncan to prison, did not share the same deep sense of devotion. He was more of an outsider, hired to restore confidence and bring stability to the office of the chief financial executive. Bill, as Gordon was known around the office, was also the only white member of BET's executive staff. In a company that was 96 percent black, he was an exception. Almost immediately, Gordon made it clear to Johnson that he had no intention of handing over any of his options. Johnson accepted Gordon's decision, not pressuring him to reconsider.

But Johnson aggressively lobbied and pressured the other five executives, telling them that he needed them to sacrifice in order to preserve and continue to pursue the company's long-term goals. "Do this for the company," Johnson urged them.

Symonds asked Johnson, "Why aren't you pressing Bill to participate?"

"I don't count Bill in this," Johnson replied.

"You don't count him?" an incredulous Symonds replied. "Why not? Because he's a white boy?"[1]

Johnson ignored the comment. But clearly, he had set different standards and rules for accepting his proposal, and that did not sit well with the other five executives as they considered the offer.

For the first and maybe only time in their lives, the executives had the opportunity to become instant millionaires. As always, they wanted to do what Johnson was requesting of them. But never before had the stakes been so large. This was their chance to get paid.

They discussed it among themselves. They wanted the company to continue to be successful, but they were also mindful of the fact that BET's first three employees—including Johnson's own sister—had been forced to sue him to get a share of the money they contended had been promised to them. These executives did not want to find themselves in the same situation. One by one, they informed Johnson that they would not give up any of their stock options.

The BET chief was incensed by their decision. In the past, all the executives had always done just as he wished. Over the years, he had not only cultivated their loyalty, he had also made them fully dependent on him, helping them to buy homes and cars or whatever they needed. "He had the golden handcuffs on us," says one of the executives.

By refusing Johnson's offer, they were boldly asserting their independence. Yet in Johnson's view, it was the ultimate betrayal, a dereliction of allegiance. Now they, too, would be members of the millionaires club—just like him. Begrudgingly, Johnson agreed to pay about $6.5 million to each of his top executives.

But there was one exception.

A few weeks before the executives were to leave for the retreat in Palm Beach, they all gathered inside the cavernous Studio 2 on BET's corporate campus for a huge companywide meeting. With most of the more than 400 employees in attendance, Johnson stood and made an announcement.

"I want to let everyone know that I just created six multimillionaires, and the only one who agreed to give back to the company was Debra Lee," he said. "In return, she will own 2 percent of the new company."

Up front in the audience, Jeff Lee, Ebron, Symonds, and Thomas leaned forward in their seats, unable to believe what they were hearing. "We were all sitting there, just shocked," recalls Symonds. "None of us had ever been offered a stake in the new company." If there was any question in their minds before, they now knew for sure that Debra Lee was valued by the boss far more than any of the rest of them.

For the next few weeks, no one spoke much about the stock option fiasco. It seemed that it was all over and done with. Getting back to business, the executives headed to Palm Beach for the retreat. For dinner the first evening, they chartered a huge boat on which they could cruise, eat, talk business, and hear the boss deliver his annual "state of the union" message.

As everyone came down to the lobby of the hotel to wait for the shuttle bus that would take them to the boat, a limousine pulled up with Johnson and Debra Lee in the backseat. The pair had been traveling together a lot lately, and Johnson now rarely shared his itinerary with his former traveling companions, Jeff Lee and Curtis Symonds.

When Johnson stepped out of the limo, Jeff Lee and Symonds walked over and began to playfully razz him about his fancy mode of transportation. But Johnson was a little uptight. He wasn't in a laughing mood. "Yo, what's up?" Jeff Lee asked. "Not much," Johnson sullenly replied.

When the shuttle bus pulled up, Symonds asked, "Bob, you're riding with us, right?"

"No, I'm riding in the limo," Johnson said as he walked back toward the car.

"What?" Symonds said. "You're kidding, right?"

"No, I'm not kidding," Johnson replied. "I'm riding in the limo."

"But, Bob," Symonds continued, "I thought the whole purpose of the retreat was for us to spend time together. I thought we were trying to build some team synergy."

But Johnson was not interested in bonding. "Debbie and I are riding in the limo," he insisted.

At that point everyone boarded the shuttle bus, except for Johnson and Debra Lee, who instead stood next to the bus debating whether they should join the others or take the limousine.

Johnson was stubborn as usual and it wasn't easy for Debra Lee to change his mind. But after about 15 minutes, with all of the vice presidents sitting on the bus watching their two top leaders debate, the two climbed aboard.

"Bob, what was all that about?" Symonds asked.

"I'll talk to you more about it at dinner," Johnson promised.

The boat was sailing off the coast of Florida and everyone was seated around a long table having drinks, eating, and talking when Johnson began his speech. Not long into his discussion he began explaining why he had decided to break with tradition and invite his lower-ranking vice presidents to the retreat.

"I'm no longer sure about the executive vice presidents who recently became millionaires," he said. "They've been taken care of now, and I'm not sure about their commitment moving forward. Those of you who are here for the first time tonight, I want you to know that this may be your opportunity to step up."

For a few more minutes, Johnson continued to harshly browbeat his executive vice presidents, criticizing their decision to get paid for all their stock options. With each word, everyone around the table grew more and more uneasy. People had mortified looks on their faces. Finally, Symonds could not take it any longer.

"What the fuck is this, Bob?" Symonds blurted out. "Is this necessary? If you've got a problem with us, why don't you pull us to the side and let's discuss the issue. Why are you discussing it in front of all of these people who weren't involved?"

The gloves were off. Johnson made it clear that he no longer had confidence in those who had devoted so many years to making his company a success. "You have shown that you're not committed to me," he said.

The discussion grew more and more heated. James Ebron stood and spoke in defense of the decision that he and his colleagues made with regard to the stock options. Jeff Lee did the same. "Bob," Lee said, "I've walked through fire for this company."[2] Others also began to weigh in. "Why aren't you proud of the fact that we've been rewarded?" one of them asked Johnson. "You told us a long time ago that if we built this company with you, one day we would get reciprocated. Now that we've received what we deserve, you're holding it over our heads."

At one point, one of the lower-ranking vice presidents, a young advertising executive, decided to speak up in support of Johnson. "Mr. Johnson," he said, "it sounds to me like some people here are not appreciative enough of what you've done for them because—" But before the young brownnoser could finish his sentence, Symonds sprang from his chair. "You shut up," Symonds told the ambitious young executive. "You don't even understand the issues."[3]

That was the way that Johnson's "state of the union" went that night. For more than an hour, there was yelling and cursing and tears.

"You could call that boat the *Titanic*," one of the executives who was on board later bemoaned. Another executive equated the experience to witnessing "a public execution."

Johnson had taken his executive vice presidents out on the high seas and made them walk the plank. "Everyone had been so close to each other," says Curtis Gadson, who was one of the up-and-coming vice presidents along on the boat ride. "That night marked the breakup of a black family."

Meanwhile, the buyout offer made by Johnson and Malone was meeting stiff resistance from shareholders. Even though the September 10 bid was 16 percent above the previous day's closing price, investors weren't happy. Most of the BET shares were held by large institutions and overseen by powerful money managers who were just about as cunning as Johnson and Malone. They knew a lowball offer when they saw one.

The largest outside shareholder, Gabelli & Company led by Mario Gabelli, filed a complaint with the Securities and Exchange Commission calling the offer "inadequate." Working behind the scenes to force Johnson to pay shareholders more, Gabelli teamed with BET's second-largest outside shareholder, Gordon Crawford's Capital Research Management.

Another institutional shareholder filed a lawsuit to block the deal, charging that it was "grossly inadequate and unfair." Wall Street began to bet that the payoff to shareholders would be a lot more than the initial $48 offer. Gabelli himself began buying up the stock, increasing his stake to over 15 percent. Within a few weeks, BET shares had shot up to $53.

Finally, investors were confirming what Johnson knew all along: BET was worth much more than the market had been tepidly valuing it at. The network now had more than 50 million viewers and was one of the 20 largest cable channels in the United States. Moreover, it was the only channel targeting African-Americans. For 13 consecutive quarters, the company had reported increases in profits. For the fiscal year that ended in July 1997, just two months before the buyout offer, BET had $154 million in revenues, $62 million in cash flow, and net income of $24 million.

Compared to other similar properties that had just been sold, Johnson's bid—which was about 13 times BET's annual cash flow—was indeed low. The cable channel known as E! Entertainment had just sold for 15 times its annual cash flow to a joint venture owned by Comcast Corporation and the Walt Disney Company. And Rupert Murdoch's News Corp. had just paid $1.9 billion, or 17 times cash flow, to purchase the Family Channel from Pat Robertson.

With their exclusive super-voting BET shares, Johnson and Malone controlled 90 percent of the voting power, a fact that made the public shareholders fearful that they would not get a fair deal. Those fears were exacerbated when the BET board, which was also essentially controlled by Johnson and Malone, appointed a so-called "special independent committee" to evaluate the offer and decide whether or not it was fair.

Delano Lewis, a BET board member and one of Johnson's best friends, headed the committee. The friendship between Lewis and Johnson went back to the days when the two worked together for Walter Fauntroy, the congressman from Washington, D.C. Lewis, who was the president of National Public Radio and the former president of the local telephone company, Chesapeake & Potomac, seemed likely to simply rubber-stamp his old buddy's lowball bid.

Lewis hired Goldman Sachs to evaluate the offer, and a few months later, in January 1998, he surprised shareholders when he announced that his independent committee had decided that Johnson's bid was "not adequate."

In response Johnson and his bankers at Salomon Brothers were forced to reevaluate their bid, and several weeks later the Johnson and Malone offer was increased to $63 per share, or a total of $378 million. Gabelli, leader of the rebellious shareholders, quickly indicated that he liked the new offer. He could push for more, but why be greedy, he said. "Bulls make money, bears make money, and pigs get slaughtered," Gabelli said, citing old Wall Street words of wisdom. In July of that year, shareholders approved the deal, which placed an implied valued of just over $1 billion on BET.

That same month, shareholders voted in favor of the offer. It may have been rocky at times, but BET had given them a nice ride. It started just seven years earlier at $17 a share, and now they were cashing out at $63.

In the new private entity, dubbed BET Holdings II, Johnson held 63 percent of the equity, Malone's Liberty held 35 percent, and Debra Lee, Johnson's trusted number two, had 2 percent. The leveraged buyout left the new firm with about $450 million in debt. But to Johnson, it was a price worth paying to reclaim full control of his company. No longer would he have to explain his vision to money managers. He could grow the company as he saw fit, without the restraints of the market.

Johnson and Debra Lee went to work, dealing with the order of power in the executive suite. Now that she was an owner, Lee could firmly assert her authority as the firm's number two executive. It was just Johnson and her at the top now, and they were always at each other's side. "You couldn't see one without the other," says one of the executive vice presidents.

Everything they did was so much in tandem that when employees talked about new orders or directions coming from up top, their sentences started with the words, "Bob and Debbie want . . ."

Some employees began to notice that the chief executive and his chief operating officer were also together quite a bit outside of the office and during after-work hours. They would join each other for dinner at the Four Seasons and other upscale places in Washington. Low-ranking BET employees would sometimes spot the two together and come into the office the next day whispering about the encounter.

When Kelli Richardson, the company's new senior vice president for marketing and communications, took a group of about 50 of her employees to Miami's South Beach for a retreat of their own, Debra Lee invited them all over one evening to her nearby oceanfront condo. The employees were a little stunned when they stepped off the elevator and into the condo and found that Lee was not there alone or with her family. She was there with Johnson. "Bob's presence created quite a buzz," says one of the employees in the group.

It wasn't long before the newly minted millionaire executive vice presidents began to see much of their power stripped away. They had always enjoyed direct communications to Johnson, but were now required to report to Debra Lee. The entire production department was taken away from Jeff Lee. He was placed in charge of new technology, a new division in which he managed only a few people.

The message was clear. And often it was not very subtle. One day, Johnson called Janis Thomas into his office and asked her, "What exactly do you do here?"

One by one, all the executive vice presidents were forced to resign. Symonds outlasted them all, but he, too, was eventually stripped of much of his responsibility. Alas, he and Debra Lee began bumping heads and one day their increasingly contentious relationship erupted into a heated argument. When it was over, Symonds was fired. True to his populist form, he marched downstairs and pulled workers together for an impromptu meeting. "The company has asked me to resign," Symonds announced. Some of the workers cried. Their link to the sixth floor executive suite was broken.

The biggest executive dismissal, however, was carried out quietly, with only a couple of people even knowing that it had occurred. Sheila Johnson had continued for several years to run corporate affairs at BET. Functioning as the executive suite's social consciousness, she had been overseeing community outreach programs and public affairs programming. But just as he did with the others, Johnson began to indicate that he no longer wanted Sheila at the company. He even stopped allowing her to use the corporate jet. Sparing not even the woman who had been with him since long before BET was conceived, Bob Johnson fired his wife. "All of us were fired," Sheila Johnson confirmed. "It got nasty, very nasty."[4]

New executives were elevated to replace the old ones, and Johnson dug in even more, seeming to grow increasingly obstinate about how the company should be run and showing even less compunction about the network's choice of shows.

Debra Lee, however, was more sensitive to the criticism and seemed to sometimes agonize over the network's bad public perception. "I'm not ready to give up on the race," she told a colleague while discussing programming changes. When she

attended a reunion at Harvard Law School in 2000, she participated in a panel discussion and was peppered with questions
and criticisms of the network.

Lee helped convince Johnson to pursue a plan that would go
a long way toward quieting the critics. In August 1999, the company announced the launch of a second BET channel that would
be filled exclusively with public affairs and family-oriented programming. The channel would be called Black Family, and it was
set up to operate as a cooperative effort among cable operators.
They would all own it and share in any profits. Black leaders applauded the idea. Lee and Johnson sent out proposals to cable
operators to participate in the venture. Since many of the operators had themselves been critical of BET's programs, this was an
opportunity for them to play a part in addressing the concerns of
their black customers. The new network, Johnson estimated,
would need an investment of $30 million and 20 million initial
cable homes to get it off the ground.

Not a single cable operator responded to the proposal. The
idea died a slow death. "We tried mightily," says Johnson. "There
were no takers whatsoever."

Meanwhile, Johnson refused to do much tinkering with his
profit machine, the main network. BET was a major success
now, and virtually no one dared to try to convince him that
things should be done any differently than they had been done
in the past. "We will not be thrown off our game," Johnson told
his staff.

But at least one employee, the talk show host Tavis Smiley,
refused to play the game. Outspoken off the air as well as on,
Smiley remained unafraid of criticizing his employer. "It gets
frustrating to be asked by young black people how I can work
for a company with no social consciousness," Smiley told
Newsweek. "I get that wherever I go, and it's something I can't
answer."[5]

Smiley's program had a stable following and he had scored major coups with interviews, such as one with Cuban president Fidel Castro and another with the media-shy musician known as Prince. But to Johnson personally, the young talk show host was an annoyance—an unruly worker who refused to accept the boss's bottom-line philosophy. "The E in BET does not stand for emancipation," Johnson allegedly told Smiley. "And it does not stand for enlightenment. It stands for entertainment."[6]

Instead of upsetting his very profitable programming mix, which was still mostly music, Johnson focused his attention on new deals to grow the company. The Internet was still in its boom days and potential investors everywhere were armed with loads of venture capital and searching for the most promising business plans.

BET had established a presence on the World Wide Web earlier when in 1996 it launched MSBET, a mostly promotional Internet site that was produced in cooperation with the Microsoft Corporation. Other African-American-oriented sites were popping up around the same time, businesses launched with private funding in hopes of cashing in either by going public—like so many Internet companies were doing—or by being acquired by a larger firm that needed a ready-made Web business aimed at African-Americans.

Herb Wilkins, the venture fund manager and former BET board member, had invested in another black-oriented Web portal known as NetNoir. Wilkins' fund, known as Syncom, had pumped more than $4 million into NetNoir, but like most Internet firms NetNoir was burning cash fast and there were no profits. Trying to save his investment, Wilkins arranged for David Ellington, the founder of the San Francisco–based firm, to meet with Johnson to discuss a possible merger of their Web-based businesses. They both knew that in the end there would be only a few successful Internet companies serving the African-American market, so a merger made good sense for both.

Ellington and Johnson easily agreed on financial terms, but they were unable to agree on who would control a merged entity. During the negotiations, Ellington proved to be a true product of the dot-com era, when young entrepreneurs were so easily swept up in their own hype that they ignored rational business principles. Even though BET was a much more established business, Ellington insisted that he could do a better job running an Internet company than Johnson could.

We can do this my way, Johnson replied, or "I'll just sit here and let your company go out of business."

After the meeting, Wilkins tried to convince Ellington to acquiesce to Johnson's terms. "Bob is going to win this because he's got the resources and you don't," Wilkins warned him. But Ellington insisted that he could compete against BET and did not need to partner with Johnson. "The guy is an asshole," Ellington told Wilkins. "Our company can kick his ass."[7]

Shortly thereafter, in August 1999, Johnson announced that BET was partnering with Microsoft, Liberty, News Corp., and USA Network to form a new African-American Internet venture, BET.com. It would replace the old MSBET, and be funded with an initial investment of $35 million, the largest amount ever devoted to a black Web business. A few other firms in the black Internet space still had a chance, but Johnson now had some of the most powerful media companies in the world as his partners. BET was guaranteed to be a formidable player in the Internet business for years to come.

Like others before him, Ellington had underestimated Johnson. The dot-com boom soon went bust, and only the strong survived. NetNoir was sold in 2001 to a Baltimore, Maryland, financial services firm for $400,000. Wilkins and other investors lost nearly all of their money, receiving only five cents for every dollar they had invested in NetNoir.

Before the dot-com economy faltered, Johnson was envisioning taking BET.com public within a couple of years. He estimated that it would quickly have a market value of about $1 billion. But to make it successful, the new BET Internet site would need exclusive content, so Johnson soon struck a deal to assist in that area. He agreed to merge BET's magazine holdings with Vanguarde Media, a fledgling publishing enterprise that owned two titles—*Honey*, which was aimed at young multicultural women, and *Impact*, a black entertainment trade publication.

The deal left BET with a 35 percent ownership stake in the combined magazine entity. An equity investment fund, Provender Capital, and Vanguarde's founder, Keith Clinkscales, held the remaining stake. The merger, however, offered solid potential for growth because Clinkscales, who had made a name for himself as the publisher who built the highly successful music magazine *Vibe*, would assume the day-to-day responsibility for BET's three titles—*Emerge*, *BET Weekend*, and *Heart & Soul*. Clinkscales, a young Harvard Business School graduate, was very much like Johnson had been 20 years earlier: a hungry media mogul in the making. If BET's magazines were ever going to turn the corner and become profitable, teaming with Clinkscales seemed to offer the best chance.

Clinkscales wasted little time proving that he, too, could make tough and unpopular decisions. He shut down *Emerge* and *BET Weekend*—both of which were showing little growth—and devoted those resources to the start-up of a new magazine, *Savoy*, an urbane lifestyle-oriented title. (But unfortunately, in 2003, after struggling with a prolonged downturn in the advertising market and weak subscriber numbers, Vanguarde was forced into bankruptcy. Most of Johnson's investment was lost.)[8]

Johnson, meanwhile, focused his attention on finding a big, transformational deal. Consolidations, mergers, and acquisitions were sweeping through the entire media industry, and like other moguls, Johnson was trying to figure out how he could jump in on the action and seize an opportunity for himself.

An opportunity seemed to present itself in October 1999, when the radio station giant Clear Channel announced that it would pay $23 billion to purchase the radio station company known as AMFM. To gain regulatory approval for the megadeal, Clear Channel had to sell more than 100 stations to avoid having too many overlapping properties in the same market. Johnson decided to try to purchase some of the discarded stations, and he teamed with Malone to raise $1 billion to fund the acquisitions.

A few months later, BET was set to buy more than 20 radio stations in 12 markets; but at the eleventh hour, when it was time to put down a nonrefundable deposit of $200 million, Johnson decided to pull out of the deal. "The multiples that we were buying at were extremely high," Johnson says. "We really didn't have radio management in place, and the debt would have just swamped us."[9]

Right about the same time, however, there was another occurrence that not only influenced Johnson's decision to cancel the radio deal, but also altered his entire vision for the future. In January 2000, the Internet power America Online announced that it would merge with the media giant Time Warner in a deal valued at over $100 billion. The news of this deal, Johnson says, was "a wake-up call."[10]

As the home of magazines, cable channels, music labels, and film studios, Time Warner owned some of the most formidable media and entertainment brands in the world. At the same time, although America Online was young, it was one of Wall Street's hottest stocks. The deal made one thing clear to Johnson and to others in the industry: Content was king. "I looked at that deal and I said, 'Okay, the game is now content.'

If you've got a proprietary brand, the smartest thing to do is beef up that brand," Johnson recalls. "Then somebody will come and buy it."[11]

It did not take long. One spring day several weeks later, John Malone received a telephone call at his office in Denver. The caller was Sumner Redstone, the wily old chairman of the entertainment giant Viacom Inc. Redstone was about to make a suggestion that would forever change Bob Johnson's life.

13

"SELLOUT!"

John Malone contacted Johnson to tell him that Sumner Redstone was interested in getting together to discuss a possible business relationship between BET and Redstone's sprawling international media company, Viacom Incorporated.

"Gee, you know we're always looking for strategic partners," Johnson said, not knowing what Redstone had in mind. "Yeah, I'll talk to him." Johnson felt certain that a major partnership of any type with Viacom, if structured correctly, would offer tremendous growth potential for the BET brand.

Viacom was one of the world's great media empires. It had been a television and production unit of CBS, but in 1971 was spun off as a separate public company after the Federal Communications Commission issued rules that prohibited the television networks from owning a financial interest in the syndication of their programs. Years later, however, the rule was overturned, opening the floodgates for networks to purchase production and syndication companies.

Redstone, a tough Boston-bred lawyer, was running his family's modest movie theater chain, National Amusements Inc., when he began investing in media and entertainment companies. He was an adamant believer in combining distribution outlets—theater chains, TV networks, video stores, bookstores, and so on—with creative content and programming. He coined the phrase "content is king," and he backed it up with his checkbook, purchasing strong content-oriented media brands as well as key distribution systems. In 1987, he bought Viacom for $3.4 billion, and then in 1994 paid $10 billion for Paramount Pictures.

By the time that Redstone contacted Malone to inquire about BET, Viacom's expansive universe included MTV, Nickelodeon, VH1, TV Land, Comedy Central, United Paramount Network (UPN), Country Music Television, Showtime, the CBS network, Simon & Schuster publishing, Blockbuster video stores, radio station giant Infinity Broadcasting, Infinity's billboard advertising business, and Paramount amusement parks.

Following up on his conversation with Malone, Johnson placed a call to Redstone's office in New York. "Let's get together," the BET chairman suggested. Redstone informed him that he would be out of the country for a couple of weeks but would call to set something up upon his return. So when Redstone arrived back in the United States he telephoned Johnson and the two men agreed to meet at Redstone's office in late May of 2000.

In addition to Redstone and Johnson, the meeting included Debra Lee and Redstone's number two at Viacom, the company's president and chief operating officer, Mel Karmazin. Johnson told Redstone that he would be interested in a strategic partnership—something that would allow him to maintain ownership control of BET while gaining the benefit of Viacom's financial resources and power in the marketplace.

But Redstone wanted more. The cable business had splintered audiences into narrowly focused niches. With its wide variety of cable holdings, Viacom already had channels that reached a broad demographic; Johnson, however, still had the first and only substantial channel targeted to African-Americans. Moreover, BET was one of the last independent cable channels that had nearly full distribution, strong cash flow, and plenty of room for improvement. A strategic partnership, Redstone said during the meeting, was of no interest to him. He did not want a minority stake in BET. He wanted to own it.

"What are your goals for BET?" Redstone asked.

"We want BET to continue to be the premium African-American media entertainment company in the country," Johnson replied.

"Well, that's my goal," said Redstone. "Let me help you."[1]

Johnson left New York pondering the idea of selling the company that he had spent the previous 20 years building. Johnson and Debra Lee contacted Malone, and together the three of them discussed Redstone's offer, contemplating what it would mean for the company and for themselves. The timing for selling seemed right, since cable channels were going for top dollar in the marketplace. And with all of the consolidation going on in the industry, they knew that in the long term it would be difficult for BET to continue to thrive as an independent company. Moreover, BET could gain economies of scale and synergy by becoming part of a much larger group of assets like those held by Viacom.

Deciding to move forward, BET hired Allen & Company, the New York investment banking boutique that specializes in media and entertainment deals. The first part of the negotiations with Viacom, deciding on a price, was relatively easy.

Like other cable deals, the sale price would be based on a multiple of BET's annual earnings before interest, taxes, depreciation, and amortization (EBITDA). "The money issue was resolved pretty quickly," recalls Johnson. "We wouldn't sell below our multiple and they wouldn't buy above their multiple." Similar cable properties had recently been selling at multiples in the low 20s. BET and Viacom agreed on a multiple of 22 times EBITDA of about $135 million. Also, Johnson, Malone, and Lee made it clear that they wanted Viacom stock, not cash, since a cash deal would have severe tax consequences. Plus with the Viacom stock, Johnson and his partners would continue to benefit as long as Viacom shares performed well.

There were still a host of issues to settle, but assuming that both sides could reach agreement, the deal would total $2.3 billion in Viacom stock, plus the assumption of nearly $600 million in long-term debt held by BET. The total purchase price: almost $3 billion!

It sounded great, but was this the best offer? The bankers at Allen & Company recommended that Johnson and Lee fly out to Sun Valley, Idaho, to attend the gathering of media and entertainment industry titans hosted there each year by the bank's leader, Herb Allen. This would give the BET executives an opportunity to test the water and see if there were other suitors interested in purchasing BET. If they were going to sell, they needed to make sure they got as good a deal as possible. A competing suitor might make a better offer or at least force Viacom to pay more.

Johnson and Lee arrived at Sun Valley and found themselves in rarefied air. Allen's Sun Valley retreat is an ultra-exclusive gathering attended by the world's major moguls. The richest man in the world, Microsoft founder Bill Gates, was there. So was the second-richest, investor Warren Buffett. There was the *Washington Post's* grande dame Katharine Graham, Disney's savior Michael Eisner, and the always colorful cable pioneer Ted Turner. The list went on and on—you name them, they were likely right there.

Even those who could not stand each other or whose companies were at war somehow seemed to make peace for a few days to enjoy the idyllic setting among central Idaho's mountains. Sun Valley was the one place where they could all gather away from the spotlight that typically shone on each of them every day. No media were allowed inside the exclusive resort. This, of course, was not a difficult rule to enforce, since all the people attending controlled the media industry. They did, however, let a photographer from the magazine *Vanity Fair* come inside and shoot a group photo each year. When the photo ran in the magazine, it was always amazing to see that so many outsized egos could actually fit within the frame of one photographer's lens.

Despite the media ban, reporters still held vigil outside the gates of the resort, scrambling for sightings of people arriving, pleading for quick interviews, and speculating about what sort of deals were being discussed inside. Everyone knew that this was a place where deals took root, since all of the dealmakers were right there.

Inside the resort, the casually dressed attendees would gather to hear presentations from company executives. They would talk business over lunch, take walks together, play tennis, and ride bikes. It was Camp Mogul.

Johnson had attended before, but he and Debra Lee were still like novelties at Sun Valley. Their bankers escorted them around and showed them off, introducing them to chief executives who might also be interested in buying BET. It was, as Lee recalled, "a beauty pageant."[2]

Among those in attendance was Gerald Levin, AOL Time Warner's chief executive officer. They talked, and according to Herb Wilkins, Johnson's longtime partner and confidant, AOL Time Warner expressed a serious interest. "Bob was talking to Warner and Viacom at the same time," says Wilkins. "It was very calculated on Bob's part." Johnson, however, says that it was just a matter of talking with "the usual suspects."

Ironically, Time Warner was the same company that several years earlier had sold its stake in BET. Now it appeared that Time Warner had taken a renewed interest in BET's demographic and in fact had pondered a major investment in a new cable start-up, New Urban Entertainment. Launched in 2000 to compete with BET, New Urban was partly owned by the musician Quincy Jones, who over the years had partnered with Time Warner in other ventures. Because of its relationship with Jones, Time Warner had agreed to give New Urban a close look, but then decided to pass. Underfinanced and lacking distribution, New Urban eventually went out of business.

Johnson's talks with AOL Time Warner ultimately did not go far, and he made the decision to fully focus his attention on the Viacom offer. It was a fortuitous turn of events. Had a deal with AOL Time Warner taken root and had Johnson received stock in exchange for ownership of BET, his fortune would have evaporated as AOL stock took its calamitous nosedive over the next couple of years.

Returning from Sun Valley, Johnson and Karmazin began moving forward to negotiate the final details. Karmazin had been the chief executive officer at CBS when Viacom purchased the network for $37 billion in 1999. A tireless executive with a caustic personality, Karmazin had earlier made his mark as a masterful salesman, building Infinity Broadcasting into a powerhouse in the radio industry before merging it with CBS.

Meeting at Karmazin's office in New York, BET and Viacom representatives hashed out the "social issues" involved in the acquisition. The first and most important of these issues was what would happen to Johnson. It was agreed that he would stay on as chief executive of the network under a five-year contract. Additionally, the two sides agreed that Debra Lee would also remain under the terms of a five-year pact.

Karmazin liked the idea of retaining the top two executives because it would allow Viacom to maintain continuity at BET and keep a management team in place that understood the network and its audience. "That's the only way I'll do it," Karmazin insisted.

Besides, they all knew that there would be some degree of public reaction to the news that a mainstream company was purchasing a major black-owned firm. So keeping Johnson and Lee around, they figured, would help Viacom deflect any criticism. "We knew that people would react because of this whole nostalgic thing about black ownership," Johnson said.

Johnson then negotiated for as much autonomy as he could get. As long as he was there, he did not want BET to become a part of Viacom's MTV group, which included MTV, VH1, and Nickelodeon. That group was headed by MTV co-founder Tom Freston, and Johnson made it clear that he did not want to report to anyone other than Redstone or Karmazin. Likewise, Lee requested that she would be required to report only to Johnson. If Johnson was to leave the company, Lee could exercise an option to leave also and still have the remainder of her contract honored. Johnson also requested that, as long as he was around, BET would continue to be headquartered in Washington, even though Viacom's other cable networks were based in New York. All of these requests were granted.

What Johnson did not get, however, was a seat on Viacom's board of directors. Even though the deal would make Johnson the company's second largest individual shareholder, Redstone and Karmazin did not concede any of the corporate governance responsibility to the BET chief. When asked about the perceived slight, Johnson pointed out that he was already on five boards and that Viacom had one black director, William Gray, head of the United Negro College Fund. "I'm pretty boarded out," Johnson claimed.[3]

On November 3, 2000, Viacom and BET jointly announced that Viacom had agreed to acquire BET Holdings II for the agreed-upon total of nearly $3 billion, consisting of about 40 million shares of Viacom's widely traded class B shares and the assumption of BET's debt. Lee, after 15 years at Johnson's side, received Viacom stock worth $46 million in exchange for her 2 percent stake in BET. Malone's Liberty Media, in return for his original $180,000 investment, received $805 million worth of Viacom shares for his 35 percent stake. And Johnson, who had started BET 20 years earlier with a $15,000 loan and now held 63 percent of the equity, received stock worth $1.44 billion!

It was a historic day. Johnson became the country's first African-American billionaire, shooting past the television talk show maven Oprah Winfrey, who at the time had a net worth that *Forbes* magazine estimated at $800 million. In a conference call with reporters and analysts, Johnson was ebullient as he discussed how BET would benefit under its new ownership. There would be opportunities to promote and market in conjunction with MTV and other Viacom channels. BET would become part of a much larger music video business, gaining greater leverage with record labels. MTV and Nickelodeon, with their large international distribution, would provide a paved path for BET to grow globally. With UPN's strong lineup of African-American sitcoms, BET might function as a secondary market for those shows. And by tapping the resources of the powerful CBS news network, BET could enhance its own news operation.

"It is an opportunity for the black community to receive more information, more entertainment, more relevant news and cultural information because of the potential of our partnership and our relationship," Johnson gushed.

In addition to the main network, which was now reaching 62 million households, Viacom's purchase also included the BET on Jazz channel and its 10 million households, the Arabesque Books romance publishing business, BET's stake in BET.com, and BET

Pictures II, the reconstituted film unit that produced made-for-television movies and documentaries.

Karmazin did not want to take all of BET's assets, since some did not fit well within Viacom's portfolio of companies. Consequently, Johnson retained his 35 percent of Vanguarde Media, the ill-fated company that held his magazine interests. He also kept the BET restaurants and nightclub, but in a separate deal he soon sold much of his interests in those properties also. Malone's Liberty Media took BET's 50 percent stake in BET Movies/Starz!, a premium movie channel that had been held in a joint venture with Liberty's Starz Encore Group.

Some people in the industry were stunned to see that Redstone and Karmazin, two of the toughest negotiators in the business, had paid such a high multiple for BET. But after taking a close look at BET, the Viacom honchos discovered what Johnson had been saying all along: The company was worth far more than outsiders realized. BET served a market that was expanding. Nielsen Media Research reported that from 1998 to 2000, black households with cable grew from 11.7 million to 12.2 million. And Target Market News, an ethnic marketing research firm, estimated that black consumers had annual spending power of more than $500 billion.

In addition to having the highest profit margins in the business, BET had lots of room for increasing its advertising rates. As a stand-alone black company, BET was never able to demand that advertisers pay rates comparable to the rates that they were paying to mainstream companies.

At the time of the acquisition, MTV, which reached 70 million households, was selling a 30-second ad for $8,000. BET, with just 8 million fewer households, was selling the same amount of ad time for a mere $1,500. "BET has been pricing itself at a discount to VH1 and MTV," Karmazin said.[4]

Karmazin said that advertisers had been discriminating against BET. By packaging BET with Viacom's other channels, he could automatically raise its ad rates to be more in line with those of its new corporate siblings. Redstone and Karmazin predicted large revenue and profit growth at BET over the next couple of years, and the network lived up to their prediction. Nevertheless, BET was now a cog in the giant's wheel—its annual revenue of less than $500 million would represent only about 2 percent of Viacom's total of $25 billion.

Mindful of the potential for backlash from BET's audience, Karmazin was careful to point out that the channel would not undergo any drastic change and it would remain independent. "I am looking forward to working with Bob and the entire BET organization as they continue to build on their extraordinary legacy as a unique and independent programming voice for the African-American community," Karmazin said in a prepared statement.[5]

It really did not matter that the Viacom and BET executives tried to spin and sugarcoat the news. As soon as the black community learned of the sale, there was an outcry. A powerful, independent media entity was no longer black-owned, and across the nation, on radio shows, on the Internet, at work, and during happy hour, people debated the significance of the sale. "Why didn't he find a black buyer?" people asked. "Does this mean the programming will finally get better?" others wondered. While some applauded Johnson's historic achievement, others derided him for "selling out."

"White companies are eying the growing black economy but can't figure out how to take control of it themselves," wrote Yemi Toure, a media critic and editor of a black media watchdog Internet site called Hype. "So they hunt for black fronts to do it for them, and hope that the black community does not notice."[6]

George Curry, the former editor of BET's *Emerge* magazine, was quoted in the *Sacramento Bee* reacting to the news: "You can have all the well-meaning people at Viacom that you can collect, yet they do not and cannot have what is a unique African-American perspective," Curry said. "BET, as we know it, is dead."

Ironically, many of the same people who had been critical of Johnson's stewardship also criticized him for selling the company. For these people, BET had been like an ill-mannered relative: nerve-racking, annoying, and even embarrassing. Nonetheless, they claimed it as their own, tolerated it, and even loved it.

"Many of us have been angry at BET for some time now," wrote Teresa Wiltz, a black staff member at the *Washington Post*. "We couldn't get with the infomercials, the endless reruns of tired sitcoms, the music videos peddling images of materialism, misogyny, and mayhem. We shook our heads at the rump-shaking hootchy mamas and the glorification of the playa lifestyle." However, Wiltz added, "It was ours."[7]

That, anyway, was the emotional illusion that Johnson had so skillfully capitalized on. While black people took ownership in his network, he gained access to their living rooms and pocketbooks. And that access had become very valuable. His viewers may have believed that BET was "ours," but when it was time to sell Johnson did not float trial balloons or engage in any pretense of trying to find a black buyer that could meet his terms. He consulted with his two equity partners, and sold.

Defending his decision, Johnson argued that he wanted a stock deal and there were no black businesses that could give him $3 billion in stock. This was a deal that only the Viacoms of the world could pull off, he said. He sought to reassure viewers that with Viacom's resources the quality of BET's programming would indeed improve. And he insisted that he and Debra Lee would continue to call the shots at the network.

To help make his case and get his message out, one month after the announcement of the sale Johnson called a group of black newspaper columnists over to BET's headquarters for dinner. He told them that BET's relationship with Viacom underscored a new paradigm for black businesses. He cited the recent 50/50 ownership agreement between the black women's media company Essence Communications and AOL Time Warner's Time Inc. He also noted that Oprah Winfrey entered a partnership with Hearst Magazines to publish her new magazine, O. Such relationships, Johnson said, were the way of the future. It was not important for businesses to remain "100 percent black-owned," he told the columnists. What was more important was to create "black value drivers." And that was what BET and these other companies had become.[8]

Like others before him, Johnson had proven the viability of the black consumer. Berry Gordy did it in the music industry, then sold his Motown label to a white-dominated firm. George Johnson did it in the hair care business, and then a white firm bought his Johnson Products. There are several other examples. Once these deep-pocketed mainstream companies recognize that there's money to be made among black consumers, they buy their way into the market. It is business. And in business, most things are for sale. There was a price at which Bob Johnson was willing to relinquish that most precious and rarest of black economic jewels—ownership. Viacom met that price.

By the time the New Year rolled around, the noise had subsided and the due diligence was completed. On January 23, 2001, Viacom's purchase of BET was quietly consummated. Johnson was now working for someone else, something he had vowed years ago was not for him. This time, however, he was the company's second largest shareholder.

Although Viacom had denied Johnson a seat at the table with the board, having BET under its umbrella gave the media giant instant diversity in its executive ranks. When executives met for their regular meetings, the presence of Johnson, Lee, or various BET division heads added a perspective that Viacom had been lacking.

Shortly after the deal was complete, Johnson was in a meeting with the chief executives of Viacom's businesses when the discussion turned toward how the various channels addressed AIDS prevention and research. "Bob talked about the impact here in the United States of AIDS with African-Americans, and what we as a company can do better than we are doing now in trying to help the situation in Africa," Karmazin said in an interview shortly after the deal closed. The enhanced diversity at the top, Karmazin added, "was a very attractive aspect" of the BET purchase. "The early indication," he said of the acquisition, "is that it's been great."[9]

Indeed, BET was fitting smoothly and easily within the Viacom corporate culture, and everything was going just fine. Then in late March, only a couple of months after the acquisition was completed, the calm was interrupted. Inside Karmazin's 52nd-floor office suite high above New York's Times Square, the telephone lines started lighting up—and would not stop. Each time the phone was answered, the caller on the other end sounded outraged. "I'd like to speak with the man who fired Tavis Smiley," the callers demanded.

At the same time, Karmazin's fax machines started going crazy. BET viewers were calling and writing letters demanding to know why the popular host of *BET Tonight* had been suddenly terminated, and also letting Karmazin know that they expected better programming under the new ownership. "The calls were a bolt out of the blue," says one Viacom executive. Karmazin was shocked. He had no idea what all the fuss was about. "I had never met Smiley," he later recalled. "I've never seen such passion."[10]

Karmazin may not have known what was going on, but

Johnson certainly did. Karmazin called down to BET's head-quarters in Washington, searching for some answers. Who was Tavis Smiley? Why was he fired? And why was everyone blaming Karmazin?

What Karmazin learned was that a rocky and long-simmering relationship between Johnson and the feisty Smiley had finally exploded. And black people across the country were being dragged into the middle of it.

After five years at BET, Smiley had been informed by Johnson that once his contract expired several months later, it would not be renewed. Smiley, an author and former Los Angeles radio talk show host, had become a prominent fixture on the network. With his huffy, inflated style, he used his television platform to preach each evening to "Black America," and he provided a nightly forum where prominent newsmakers, politicians, and activists could appear as his guests. Smiley's *BET Tonight* did not have great ratings—while the network averaged about 375,000 households viewing at any given time, Smiley's show averaged less than half that much—but it gave the programming lineup an intellectual counterbalance to the mindless videos, infomercials, and comedy.

During much of his time at the network, however, Smiley clashed with Johnson. Both men were headstrong and egocentric, and they disagreed over discussion topics on Smiley's show and over the content of other BET programs.

Primarily, the two clashed because Smiley was a star. An outspoken advocate for social justice and racial equality, Smiley had been named by *Time* magazine as one of America's 50 most promising leaders. Then once he began appearing on the network each night, he quickly became the most recognizable face on BET. When famous guests like Johnnie Cochran or Cornell West appeared on *BET Tonight*, it was as if Smiley was among his equals, as he referred to such people as "my good friend."

Whereas Johnson had a hard time gaining respect among the black intelligentsia, Smiley was embraced. He received National Association for the Advancement of Colored People (NAACP) image awards; he demanded to be paid well; and he demanded that his show be moved from Washington to Los Angeles, against Johnson's wishes. And even after forcing the network to concede to such demands, Smiley still maintained his independence and publicly criticized BET when he felt like doing so.

Before Smiley, at BET there had never been a star any bigger than Johnson himself. The network had been a farm system for talent. It did not pay a lot, and once people became stars they left for greener pastures. Privately, Johnson complained of Smiley's prima donna behavior. He maintained that people came on Smiley's show not because of the host himself, but because BET gave them a platform. Johnson felt that anyone could be the host and enjoy the same success as Smiley.

But Smiley did manage to snag big interviews. In 1998, he convinced the taciturn artist known as Prince to come out of his shell during an exclusive interview. And the following year, Smiley traveled to Cuba to interview the Communist country's legendary leader, Fidel Castro. As fate would have it, it was in fact a big interview that became the final straw in the ongoing dispute between Smiley and Johnson.

Early in 2001, Smiley was locked in bitter contract renewal talks with BET. At the same time, Smiley was granted a highly sought exclusive interview with Sara Jane Olson, aka Kathleen Ann Soliah, a former Symbionese Liberation Army fugitive who was on trial for her role in a bomb-planting incident that had taken place two decades earlier. Smiley conducted the interview and sold it to the ABC network. On March 1 it appeared on ABC's *Primetime Live*.

Although Smiley's contract allowed him to pursue such inde-

pendent projects, Johnson was angry that Smiley did not first offer the interview to BET. Moreover, now that BET was a part of
the company that owned CBS, it seemed inappropriate for a BET
star to appear on a competitor's network.

Johnson had had enough of his independent-minded star. He
decided that when Smiley's contract expired in September, it
would not be renewed. But instead of having someone personally
break the news to Smiley, BET sent a faxed announcement to
Smiley's agent.

BET, however, was not the only megaphone that Smiley had.
He was also a regular commentator on the *Tom Joyner Morning
Show*, which was syndicated by ABC Radio Networks and aired
on more than 120 stations. Smiley went on Joyner's show and
complained about the manner in which he was being terminated
from BET. "After five years could not one person have picked up
the phone to call me personally?" Smiley said.

With that, Joyner went into action. A legend in radio, Joyner
had earned the nicknames "Fly Jock" and "Radio Iron Man" when
he spent eight years traveling 1,600 miles round-trip each day
between Dallas and Chicago, doing shows in both cities. Not
only was he one of the radio industry's highest-paid personalities—in 1993 he signed a five-year, $15 million contract—he
was also one of its most powerful.[11]

Joyner believed in using his show, which included music,
comedy, and news, as a platform for activism. He has raised millions of dollars by urging his listeners to support historically
black colleges. And together, Joyner and Smiley had earlier
taken to the airwaves and prompted listeners to telephone
Christie's auction house in New York to complain about a
planned auction of antique posters advertising rewards for runaway slaves. As a result, the auction was canceled. They used a
similar tactic to force the computer retailer CompUSA to adver-
tise on black media, pointing out the large number of black con-

sumers who purchased the store's products. So when Smiley announced that he was being fired from BET, the machinery was primed, and he and Joyner immediately took aim at the top—BET's new parent, Viacom.

On the air, Joyner gave out Karmazin's telephone and fax numbers, and his e-mail address. He urged listeners to contact Karmazin and denounce Smiley's dismissal. "BET has silenced a great journalist and a great advocate who has kept millions of black Americans informed on issues that mainstream media tends to ignore," Joyner told his listeners.[12]

With Karmazin's telephone lines going crazy and Smiley on the radio bad-mouthing BET, Johnson grew incensed. He decided that he would not wait for Smiley's contract to expire several months later. Instead, Johnson fired Smiley, effective immediately.

Now things really got ugly. Tavis and Joyner discussed whether or not they should press the issue further on the air. According to Joyner, "Tavis didn't want to seem like a disgruntled former employee." But Joyner felt that it was necessary to seize the moment and focus attention on BET and its programming. "It had started out with the firing of Tavis," Joyner later recalled. "But now it was much larger."[13]

Joyner took to the air, urging his listeners to continue to storm Viacom's telephone lines. "Let's tell Viacom what you really expect in your network," he told listeners. And many of the eight million people who tune in weekly to Joyner's show followed his orders. The response was overwhelming. In Detroit, a group of 162 religious leaders voted to write and call Karmazin. In New York, the Reverend Al Sharpton threatened to demonstrate in front of BET's Harlem studio. In Los Angeles, protestors gathered outside an event where Karmazin was speaking.

Because Smiley's interview with Olson had aired on ABC instead of CBS, many people speculated that Karmazin had ordered Johnson to fire Smiley. Karmazin and Johnson vehemently denied this; however, the viewpoint that ran rampant was that Smiley's firing had confirmed BET viewers' worst fears: The network was no longer controlled by black people. The white men at Viacom were calling the shots at BET.

"What was being said was that Bob did not have the authority to fire someone because he was now working for someone who was white," Karmazin later recalled. "I was sort of offended that people would insult Bob by thinking that he would allow me to do something like that. Bob hired Tavis Smiley. Bob fired Tavis Smiley."[14]

Nevertheless, Johnson was called "a pawn" and accused of carrying out Karmazin's orders. On the popular black-oriented web site Urban Expose, a stream of chatters weighed in. "Bob made himself look like a yes-man to the powers that be at Viacom," wrote one person. Another one called Johnson "the 2001 version of the dude who drove Miss Daisy around."

Finally, in an attempt to quiet the firestorm, Johnson personally took to the airwaves. Appearing on Smiley's former show, he explained that although Viacom owned the network, he remained in charge and that firing Smiley was his decision alone. It was strange television. For an hour, BET viewers watched as Johnson answered questions posed humbly by Smiley's successor, Cheryl Martin. It came across as strained and contrived, even though Johnson was candid about his difficulties in dealing with Smiley. "The relationship was fraught with tension," Johnson said in the aired program. "And I didn't want this relationship to go any further."

Johnson even took questions from callers. He was so determined to emphasize that he was in control of the network that he came across as arrogant. When one caller asked Johnson if he had become a "front man" for Viacom, the BET chief responded tersely: "I'm absolutely calling the shots. I make too much money to be a front man."

After Johnson's appearance, Joyner's listeners persisted with their calls and letters. Repeatedly, Johnson telephoned Joyner, who was based in Dallas, and asked him to call off the campaign. But Joyner was now insisting that he be allowed to meet with Karmazin to discuss the quality of programming on BET. "Bob, this is really not about you and Tavis and your conflicts with him. This is really about how BET represents black people," Joyner recalls telling Johnson. "This is not going to go away."

Finally, Johnson arranged a conference call with himself, Debra Lee, Joyner, and Karmazin on the line. "Look," Karmazin began, according to Joyner, "Bob is one of the major stockholders in this company. I can't make Bob do anything. I essentially work for him," Karmazin continued, perhaps stretching reality a bit. "Bob is going to do what Bob is going to do."

Joyner urged Karmazin to take note of how passionate people were about BET. "You can tell from this situation that black people want more, and no one is giving it to them," Joyner said. "If you show black Americans that you want their business, and you care about their community, they will be very loyal."

With that, Karmazin told Joyner what he needed to hear. "Bob now has the resources to do whatever he wants to do with that network," Karmazin said. "Whatever he wants to do to make that network better, he has my support."[15]

After the conference call, Joyner called off the radio campaign, assuring his listeners that Viacom had gotten the message. He told them to wait and watch closely to see if the network improved under its new owner. Smiley left BET and eventually landed as a host on National Public Radio.

Karmazin confessed that he had never witnessed such a profound reaction from viewers or listeners in all his years in the broadcast business. Always the salesman, though, Karmazin immediately capitalized on the controversy. "We took all of those e-mails," he said, "and used them to show advertisers the kind of response that BET can get." For everyone inside Viacom's corporate suite, the whole episode was a fiery introduction to the world of Black Entertainment Television. Some of them were left wondering, "What have we gotten ourselves into?"

HE GOT GAME

During late summer each year, rich people from around the United States and some foreign countries load up their prize horses, English riding gear, and highly paid trainers, and head for the east end of Long Island, New York.

The annual Hampton Classic Horse Show is a world of wealth unto itself. For an entire week, the festival of equestrian exhibitions and competitions attracts movie stars, models, and moguls to a vast swath of flat farmland converted into a mini city of stables, riding rings, boutiques, and luxuriously catered meals. The regulars who mingle under the huge white tents make up a Who's Who of business, fashion, and entertainment. There is Calvin Klein, Christie Brinkley, Steven Spielberg, Kathleen Turner, the Dolans of Cablevision, and the Bloombergs of the financial information empire bearing their name. And of course, there are the Johnsons of Black Entertainment Television.

It is a long way from Hickory, Mississippi.

Just as they had been doing for many years, the entire Johnson family and their staff from Salamander Farm traveled to the Hamptons for the 2002 show, where 16-year-old Paige Johnson was competing and defending her championship in a number of events. Bob and Sheila are fixtures among the horsey set now. Their daughter is a star rider and they are major benefactors of this and other equestrian competitions. Sitting under a tent between events on a moist, brisk afternoon, Sheila is constantly interrupted by people who come by to fawningly say hello. "You have a wonderful daughter, really wonderful," gushes one woman. "She looks so beautiful also." A while later, Bob arrives with their 12-year-old son, Brett, who is wearing a Michael Jordan Wizards jersey, a look he prefers over the polo shirts and boots that every other kid at the horse show seems to be wearing. By all indications, the Johnsons are living the good life. But they are living it apart.

Although they are both attending the horse show to support their daughter, Sheila and Bob are in the final months of divorce proceedings and their relationship is as frosty as a mint julep. (Several months earlier, the couple squared off when Bob Johnson gave Paige a $48,000 Mercedes two-seat sports car for her 16th birthday. Sheila insisted that the car was too small and too fast for a young, inexperienced driver. She took the birthday gift and donated it as a raffle prize for a local fund-raiser.[1])

As they take their places in the bleachers to watch Paige compete at the Hampton Classic, Sheila sits in the front row along with Brett, and Bob climbs the stairs to sit 50 yards away in the top row. "There is a sadness in me," Sheila confides during an interview with me that same day. "I just feel so bad. But I have to go on with my life."

Wearing rimless specs, a yellow rain slicker, and a white baseball cap with the word "Courageous" inscribed on the front, Sheila is calm and forthright as she assesses her 33-year marriage. She still praises her soon-to-be ex-husband. "He's a brilliant businessman," she says. "And there will be a part of me that will always love him." But, she reveals, extramarital affairs "were his biggest problem. He has got a body count."

Bob's relationship with Debra Lee, whom Sheila had been so close to over the years, has left her stunned. "That affair with Debra just hurt me more than anything, because I knew her, and I couldn't believe she would do that," Sheila says. "There was obviously a side of her I never knew. . . . I find the whole thing tragic."[2]

Yet when it comes to getting even and salving the wounds, there is nothing as effective as splitting up a fortune. Though the Johnsons kept their divorce proceedings tightly sealed, close associates say that Sheila walked away with cash and stock. Additionally, she kept the Middleburg, Virginia, farm and the home and riding facility in Wellington, Florida.

By the time the divorce was finalized in late 2002, Sheila, at age 53, had focused her attention on a major purchase of her own. She spent $7 million to buy a 349-acre tract of land formerly owned by the late diplomat and socialite Pamela Harriman. Located near Salamander Farm on the border of Middleburg, the tract was about to be purchased by developers intending to subdivide and fill it with modest homes. Urged on by a local environmental group opposed to the housing development, Sheila stepped in, offered a 30-day cash settlement, and the land was hers.

Shortly after the purchase, she donned her boots, brought along a group of friends, and hiked across the property, which was covered with woods, streams, and trails from the mounted hunts that had passed through for years. "I can't believe I own this," she marveled, as she looked around and savored her surroundings. "It is so beautiful." Suddenly she had an epiphany. "This would make a beautiful place for an inn," Sheila recalls thinking. "So I called my lawyer."

In 2003, she broke ground on the Salamander Inn and Spa, a 40-room luxury resort, conference center, and equestrian facility. She has permanently placed her mark on the old-money community of about 600 residents. She donated $3 million to build the Sheila C. Johnson Performing Arts Center at the nearby Hill School, the private academy Brett attends.

Sheila, in fact, became a major philanthropist, with her generous donations going far beyond the Middleburg community. She gave $1 million to the State University of New York at Morrisville. In turn, the school established an institute in her name to encourage diversity through scholarships and fellowships. And in 2003, she donated $7 million to New York's Parsons School of Design, where she also served as a board member. Additionally, Sheila Johnson took on the presidency of the Washington International Horse Show, a major event on the equestrian circuit. She joined the boards of the United States Equestrian Team, which chooses the Olympic team; USA Equestrian, the sport's governing body; and the International Centre for Missing and Exploited Children; and she became a spokesperson for the National Campaign to Prevent Teen Pregnancy. And after all that, she designed a line of linens bearing the Salamander Farm name, and began attempting to sell them as an upscale brand of merchandise.

"I have to go on now," Sheila says, as if reminding herself not to look back. She repeats those words, like a mantra.

Even before he had completed the sale of BET to Viacom, Bob Johnson had new ventures capturing his imagination. His presence as a board member at major corporations was creating new and exciting investment opportunities for him. Being in the boardroom was putting Johnson in "the deal flow," as he liked to call it.

Johnson was on the board of the airline US Airways when Stephen Wolf, the chairman of the company, approached him. "Bob, I got this idea," Johnson recalls Wolf saying. US Airways was struggling financially. Moving to save the company, Wolf had entered talks to merge US Airways with United Airlines, in a deal valued at nearly $12 billion. But both carriers were too dominant in the Washington region, and government regulators were sure to reject any merger that formed a monopoly. So to create more competition and satisfy antitrust concerns, Wolf suggested that Johnson take the overlapping routes and services in the region and start his own airline. "That appealed to Steve because one, it solved the regulatory problem," Johnson says. "Two, it added a tremendous political asset on his table because of who I was and because of the credibility I had in the political spectrum."[3]

As a result, in May 2000, Johnson announced the formation of DC Air, a regional airline that would operate out of Washington and serve 44 markets. Owned and headed by Johnson, the new airline would make Johnson an instant player in the rough-and-tumble airline business, where many fortunes have evaporated in the clouds. Johnson, however, was offered very attractive terms. For an initial investment of about $225 million, he would receive 222 slots, or takeoff and landing rights, at Washington's Reagan International Airport. Johnson predicted that the airline would have annual revenues of $400 million and be profitable after its first year.[4] His planned 144 daily departures were mostly on routes that were already generating a handsome profit. Making the deal even more attractive, Johnson sold 49 percent of his new carrier to American Airlines, which was kicking in $82 million in cash, additional planes, and crew members. DC Air would make Johnson the first African-American to own a major airline. This was big.

But DC Air would fly only if the merger of United and US Airways was approved by the Department of Justice. Despite the planned spin-off of routes to Johnson's company, the proposed deal, which would make United the largest airline in the world, was met with immediate opposition from consumer groups and government officials.

In the summer of 2001, as the Justice Department prepared to issue its ruling on the merger, Johnson was busy using his political connections and seasoned lobbying skills to help win approval of the deal. On the day before the decision was rendered, a telephone call he received at his office made it apparent that he had worked his contacts at the highest level.

"Hello, Mr. President," Johnson said casually. Speaking to the former president, Bill Clinton, Johnson briefly discussed the pending decision and promised, "I'll keep you posted." He ended the call in a chummy, far less formal manner. "Yeah man," Johnson said to Clinton. "We'll see."[5]

Within hours, the Justice Department announced that it was rejecting the merger of US Airways and United Airlines. Consequently, DC Air was grounded before a single plane ever left the ground.

But other investment opportunities were also materializing. As a result of his seat on the board of Hilton Hotels Corporation, in December 2000 Johnson was offered the chance to purchase seven Homewood Suites franchises from Hilton. Seizing the opportunity, he formed a limited liability corporation bearing his initials, RLJ Development, to run the hotel business, and paid $95 million to acquire the properties. The new firm aggressively sought expansion opportunities, spending an additional $26 million to purchase a Courtyard by Marriott in Baltimore's Inner Harbor. By 2003, Johnson's development firm had landed on *Black Enterprise* magazine's list of the top 100 black-owned industrial or service firms. The magazine reported that RLJ Development, ranked at number 71, had gross revenues of $49.4 million.[6]

Still, Johnson was searching for something bigger. BET no longer presented a real challenge, and besides, Debra Lee was in charge of the day-to-day operation, anyway. "The challenge for me is finding something to do that will, you know, keep me young, and have some fun," Johnson said in 2001. "Because I've done this for 20 years so I know how to do it. And I don't want to step on Debra's toes as to how she does it. So I'm always looking for things that will be of interest to do. And fortunately I am in a position to take advantage of most of it coming my way."[7]

Johnson made investments in other businesses, including

Internet lottery games on Caribbean islands and a stake in a small Maryland-based jazz music recording company.

What he still longed for, however, was to become the owner of a pro sports team.

By 2002, he had teamed up with the owner of the Washington Redskins football team, Daniel Snyder, in a bid to purchase the Montreal Expos baseball team and move the ailing franchise to Washington. The team was valued at about $225 million and was the property of major league baseball's other 29 owners, who wanted to either sell the franchise or shut it down. With the exception of one Japanese owner, baseball's ownership ranks were still all white. Even though there were competing groups vying for the Expos, Johnson was confident that with his money and background, he was the top contender. "If you get into a beauty contest, I win," he told USA Today.[8]

Around the same time, Johnson contacted the owner of the Charlotte Hornets basketball team, George Shinn, to let him know that he was interested in buying the National Basketball Association (NBA) team. Local fans had grown to dislike Shinn, who fought with city officials over a potentially lucrative new stadium and had been involved in a widely publicized sexual harassment case. Attendance at games dropped, and taxpayers expressed unwillingness to fund a new stadium as long as Shinn was the team owner. Frustrated, Shinn threatened to move the team to New Orleans. In response, Johnson stepped in and gained the support of local business leaders who were working to keep the team in Charlotte. Still, Shinn rejected Johnson's offer to buy the Hornets, and when the 2001–2002 season ended, the Hornets packed up their basketballs and moved to the Bayou State.

It wasn't the first time that Shinn had rejected Johnson. In 1999, Johnson and NBA legend Michael Jordan separately pursued the Hornets franchise. However, they were both turned down when Shinn chose to sell only a minority stake in his team.[9]

Even with all his money, Johnson was finding time and again that breaking into the ultra-exclusive club of team owners was extremely difficult.

With the Hornets gone and the people of Charlotte still expressing a willingness to build a new stadium for a new team, a fresh opportunity began to take shape. The NBA's 29 team owners began discussing the possibility of expanding the league by a single team, with the new franchise going to Charlotte. Johnson began lobbying the owners. At least one owner, Mark Cuban of the Dallas Mavericks, was opposed to adding another team to the league. Even though the existing teams would split the fee that the new franchise would pay to enter the NBA, not everyone was convinced that the league should further dilute its product. Johnson telephoned Cuban, a young owner who struck it rich by selling his Internet company during the tech boom. Never one to mince words, Cuban told Johnson, "I like you, Bob, but I don't want another team in the league. Go out and buy a team."[10]

Despite such opposition, the league's owners voted to add the 30th team to the NBA. The new team owner would have to buy the franchise for a price set by the league. In order to get the best price possible for the new team, league officials first negotiated the terms of the stadium with Charlotte officials. It was a good package: The city would finance the construction of the $265 million, 18,500-seat arena, conveniently located in uptown Charlotte close to the corporations that buy the lucrative luxury suites. The plan called for 50 to 70 luxury suites, priced at about $125,000 each per year.[11] The owner of the team would operate the facility under a 25-year lease and keep all revenue from ticket sales, luxury suites, and other events such as concerts. This was especially important for a prospective owner like Johnson, who had strong connections in show business and could likely turn the facility into a thriving entertainment complex.

Because of the attractive stadium deal and the strong fan base in Charlotte (the Hornets led the league in attendance during the late 1980s and early 1990s before falling out of favor), the NBA set the asking price of the franchise fee at $300 million, more than twice what was paid in 1994 for the Toronto and Vancouver franchises, the league's last expansion teams.

The owner selection committee came down to two competing bidders: Johnson and a group headed by a Boston businessman, Steve Belkin, and including the Boston Celtics legend Larry Bird. Belkin and Bird were planning to buy the franchise with three sources of financing: one-third coming from Belkin, one-third from a Boston-based investment group, and one-third from a Charlotte-based group. Johnson, with his deep pockets, would simply write a check for the entire $300 million, and then later sell a minority stake to Charlotte-based investors. Nevertheless, going up against Bird, one of the greatest ever to lace up the sneakers, would not be easy.

To bolster his chances of besting Bird, Johnson turned to his powerful friends in high places. According to Federal Election Commission records, in October 2002, a couple of months before the NBA franchise owner was to be selected, Johnson donated $1 million to the Democratic National Committee. It wasn't long before he got a few favors in return.

U.S. Senator John Edwards, the North Carolina Democrat who was beginning to mount a run for the White House, telephoned Jerry Colangelo, the Phoenix Suns owner and chairman of the NBA's board of governors. Edwards told Colangelo that selecting Johnson "would send a real positive signal to African-American youth."[12]

At the same time, Democratic National Committee chairman Terry McAuliffe did his part. McAuliffe was an acquaintance of Joe Maloof, the owner—along with his brother—of the Sacramento Kings. According to *Black Enterprise* magazine, at Johnson's urging, McAuliffe lobbied Maloof, who was on the NBA expansion committee charged with selecting the new team owner. Additionally, Johnson reached out to Richard Parsons, who was now the chief executive officer of AOL Time Warner, and even to former president Bill Clinton. He asked them to contact league officials on his behalf. "I basically went to these individuals to say 'Make my case to the NBA,' " Johnson said.[13]

Johnson also got his own chance to personally make his case. On December 16, 2002, the two competing groups traveled to New York, where the NBA is headquartered. There, they made one-hour presentations and were interviewed by the league's expansion committee. According to NBA sources, Johnson talked about his proven success in business and his financial stability. He outlined how he would market and manage the team, and how he planned to make the franchise a success. The last point he made to the committee, Johnson later recalled, was about the lack of diversity in their ranks. "I wanted to assure them that I wasn't asking for this franchise because I'm African-American, but that any organization that had 80 percent plus employees of a particular racial group must consider diversity," Johnson was quoted as saying.[14]

Two days later Johnson was at the NBA Store on Fifth Avenue, standing before a phalanx of cameras and microphones as the NBA commissioner, David Stern, and Colangelo formally announced the league's selection. The Charlotte franchise was awarded to Johnson! Finally, Bob Johnson had realized his dream. Finally, the color barrier in the ranks of professional sports ownership had been broken.

Surprised that the Bird group was defeated, many people were quick to attribute the selection solely to Johnson's race. But this was no affirmative action. Clearly, race was a consideration, but Johnson was the most attractive bidder for several reasons, most of all because his team would be fully controlled by him.

League officials preferred having a single owner with a clear majority stake. In the past, when a team had multiple owners with equal voices, it was often difficult for them to reach decisions on issues. "The fact that he's an African-American was a plus; it was a by-product," Colangelo said.[15]

Other blacks had held small minority percentages in various teams, but Johnson was the first black with controlling ownership. It was not discrimination within the league that had prevented it from happening earlier. It was basic economics. And economics also guaranteed that Johnson's entry would not open any floodgates. Johnson was in the club now, but the club was still reserved for the ultrarich.

With his son Brett at his side, Johnson was filled with pride at the press conference. As he spoke, he was emphatic about his qualifications. "I feel that people should be judged by their character and not, as Martin Luther King said, the color of their skin," Johnson offered. "I feel what I brought to the table was my ability and my skill as an individual, my ability to identify talented people who help me build organizations like I have with BET."

With his new team set to begin playing in the fall of 2004, Johnson had more than a year and a half to prepare. Putting his pursuit of a baseball team on the back burner, he focused his attention on his new basketball franchise.

A few months after buying the franchise, Johnson was in New York at the World Congress of Sports, an annual conference of sports business executives. Participating in a panel discussion entitled "The Powers That Be," Johnson was joined by Colangelo and Cuban. As he sat on a stage overlooking the Starlight Ballroom inside the landmark Waldorf Astoria, Johnson surveyed the room, which was packed with more than 250 executives. More than 90 percent of them were white.

"Look at this room. It has a demographic," Johnson told the audience, as some of them shifted nervously in their seats. "Look at the guys out there playing and creating the excitement. There is a demographic." The two demographics "are different," he said. "In Charlotte we're going to hire the best talent we can find, and some of that will be African-Americans who haven't had the opportunity for management elsewhere."

One of his first moves was to hire former New York Knicks executive Ed Tapscott as executive vice president and chief operating officer. Tapscott was also married to the former BET executive vice president Janis Thomas. The hiring underscored the fact that business was business with Johnson. Even though he and Thomas had parted ways not on great terms, Johnson still maintained close contact with Tapscott and trusted that he was the best man to run the team. While Tapscott went to work building the basketball organization, his wife stayed in the background, harboring mixed emotions for her old boss.

Johnson began laying out his plan for making the franchise a success. In addition to the NBA team, his purchase also included the women's professional team, the Charlotte Sting. With the two pro teams and a host of other high school and college sporting events in the region, Johnson prepared to launch a regional sports channel. This was an industry that he knew well. If successful, a regional channel would serve as a marketing platform for the team and generate lucrative fees from cable and satellite operators that carried the channel.

To help make the team attractive in the region, Johnson vowed to "look for players who can be participants in the community." Playing the game well would not be enough, he said. "If you create a whole team of villains, people will be turned off. . . . We've go to find the heroes, who people want to go on the crusade with. . . . We've got to become Charlotteans."[16] To immediately bolster the team's reputation in the community—and recoup a percentage of his investment—Johnson sold a minority stake in the franchise to a disparate group of about a dozen local business leaders.

As a new owner, Johnson would have the benefit of building his team around the league's latest collective bargaining rules. Like portfolio managers, owners must now manage their players and their contracts skillfully in order to maximize talent but avoid the costly luxury tax that teams must pay if their annual player salaries exceed the $50 million range. Teams that stay below the range share the revenues from the tax. Many teams were locked into existing contracts that made it difficult to avoid the tax. Johnson, however, could build from scratch around the new rules.

In an industry where many teams operate at an annual deficit, Johnson insisted that he would run a profitable franchise. "I would not be in this business if I was going to lose money," he told *Vibe* magazine.[17] But the pressure to win is enormous in sports, and it can push an owner to the brink. As one NBA executive said, "The fans don't walk up and congratulate you for running a profitable team."

It wasn't long before Johnson was faced with his first major personnel decision. He entered into talks with Michael Jordan, the sports' greatest icon, about becoming a minority investor and executive with the team. Jordan was just leaving an ugly situation with the Washington Wizards. He had risked his personal legacy to come out of retirement and play for the team, helping to resurrect the hapless franchise. When Jordan joined the Wizards, he had believed that his role—first as a minority owner, then as general manager and player—would lead to him eventually becoming the team's majority owner. Instead, when the season ended and he retired from the court to return full-time to the front office, he received a stunning rebuke from the team's majority owner, Abe Pollin. The veteran of the NBA's ownership ranks unceremoniously fired Jordan, the game's greatest player ever.

With Jordan's ego bruised, he and Johnson began flirting with the idea of teaming up. But while bringing the basketball king to the team would have been an attraction for fans, it would be costly for Johnson, as he would have to share the spotlight and the team's equity. It eventually became evident that Jordan really wanted an opportunity that would allow him to be—like Johnson—a major owner in a team, so the talks ended. This was Bob Johnson's team. It was not big enough to accommodate two legends.

Any lingering doubts that this new franchise belonged to Johnson were erased in June 2003 when he joined Charlotte city officials at a street festival to announce the team's official name: the Charlotte Bobcats. Even though the sleek and fierce feline is indigenous to the Carolinas, everyone familiar with the owner and his self-centered motives joked that only "Bob" Johnson would name a team after himself.

ONE NATION
UNDER A GROOVE

T he Los Angeles city council chamber is majestic. Lined on each side by marble columns and dark, polished wooden benches, there is an august air about the room. The only hint of the contemporary city outside is the cutting-edge flat panel television screens that sit in each aisle, displaying a listing of the day's proceedings. On the morning of June 25, 2002, the screens read "BET Day," and as the council members trickled into the room, Robert Johnson was already seated in the front row.

Standing out in stark contrast to the black, gray, and navy suits filling the chamber, Johnson was regal in his finely tailored off-white suit, white shirt, and white necktie. A black uniformed security guard walked over to introduce himself to the BET founder. A city council member, also black, followed. One of them whipped out a small camera and Johnson, gracious as ever, posed for a few photos with the men. They shared a few laughs and slaps on Johnson's back—the kind of backslaps that conveyed the pride they felt in meeting one of their own who had reached the pinnacle of success.

Around the same time, a distinguished panel of black intellectuals and leaders gathered in Philadelphia for a televised forum on the state of black America, hosted by the deposed BET star, Tavis Smiley. Referring to Johnson, who was not present, one panelist rhetorically quipped, "How does it feel to be a billionaire with no power?" The remark elicited a roaring applause from the hundreds of people in the audience. Even though the comment was not really true—Johnson obviously has tremendous power—the response illustrated the fiercely negative sentiments that some people harbor for the BET founder.

This is the conflicted legacy of Robert Louis Johnson, a man who has gained so much and made so many proud, yet in the process sacrificed the admiration of others. As an entrepreneur, his accomplishments are undeniable. His network demonstrated the economic viability of programming and marketing to the African-American audience. More than a media network, the business that Johnson created and built has become the backbone upon which thousands of other African-Americans have risen to prominence.

Musicians, record labels, comedians, and other entertainers owe much of their success to Johnson and BET. A primary tool for the marketing of black culture, BET now reaches over 75 million U.S. homes. Thanks in part to the network, America's urban culture is transcending racial and economic boundaries. All forms of African-American expression, from music to fashion, comedy, and religion, are now a vibrant influence on the lives of all races of people in cities, suburbs, and rural regions. Across the nation, teenage kids get out of school in the afternoon, go home, and turn on BET. In fact, the network's afternoon live video countdown, *106th and Park*, recently surpassed MTV's similar offering, *Total Request Live*, in the ratings during the same time slot.

But BET's tremendous influence is also the reason that it attracts criticism. As the primary purveyor of black images on television, BET represents blackness. And for many people, that representation is far too narrow, and far too lascivious. As Michael Eric Dyson, an author and professor in African-American studies at the University of Pennsylvania, puts it, "When you're in the public sphere controlling the representation of the black culture, the image of black people is at stake. That channel could give us more intellectual and social content, documentaries, and a lot of programming geared toward the difficult circumstances of black people. But all of that is largely absent. What we have left is the powerful image of black people as entertainers and purveyors of erotic delight."[1]

Johnson will be always be regarded by some as a sort of postmodern robber baron, a hip-hop version of the nineteenth-century capitalists like Andrew Carnegie and J. P. Morgan—men who built fortunes through ironfisted ruthlessness. And just as those empire builders did in their later years, Johnson is smoothing his image. He preaches the virtues of being a "community-oriented" NBA owner, and has become a generous philanthropist. In 2003, he donated $3 million to help build the National Underground Railroad Freedom Center. The Cincinnati, Ohio–based museum, geared toward promoting racial understanding, planned to name a theater in Johnson's honor.[2]

Johnson did not build a legacy of acclaimed and inspirational television content, but he has inspired many others to emulate his entrepreneurial prowess. His ways are the ways of the capitalist, guided by a simple, singular principle. "I am a businessman," his oft-repeated mantra goes. As such, he had the right to run his network as he saw fit. His eventual decision to sell the network was based on pure, sound business principles. The time was right. The price was right. It was not personal. It was not emotional. It was business. BET will not be the last major African-American–owned television company. It was only the first.

A couple of years after being purchased by Viacom, with Johnson and Lee still at the helm, BET veered more toward pure entertainment, eliminating much of its news and public affairs programming. Even the long-running *Teen Summit*, Sheila Johnson's personal favorite, was canceled. The network added documentaries on entertainers and their lifestyles, animated adult comedy, and reruns of the critically acclaimed drama *Soul Food*, which first aired on another Viacom channel, Showtime. But mostly, BET remained geared toward music videos.

Johnson had been insisting for a long time that BET could not "be all things to all people." And after years of thriving with virtually no competition, BET's monopoly was being threatened by a couple of new players. One of the new channels, the Major Broadcasting Cable (MBC) network, was owned by a rich and powerful Florida-based trial attorney, Willie E. Gary. His network promised to focus on "intelligent, family-oriented programming," but as an independent cable channel, MBC struggled during its first few years to get distribution beyond about 10 million households.

A second and more threatening competitor emerged in 2003, when Radio One Inc., the urban radio station company controlled by the black mother-and-son team of Cathy L. Hughes and Alfred C. Liggins, announced that it was partnering with the cable system giant Comcast to launch a new black-oriented channel. TV One, as the new channel was dubbed, had strong potential because Comcast was the nation's largest cable system with more than 20 million subscribers. Just as BET in its infancy had Malone's TCI cable systems to gain distribution, TV One had Comcast. The new channel aimed to grab a hefty share of the disenfranchised viewers who believed that BET's programming was thin and geared toward teens and young adults. "We will be more lifestyle oriented toward urban consumers over the age of 25," Liggins promised in an interview.[3] Still, it was expected to take several years for TV One to build an audience the size of BET's.

Johnson was not personally sweating the new competition. With Debra Lee running the company on a daily basis and having made his fortune, he focused on putting his basketball team together and on the enviable problems that only the rich must cope with. He campaigned aggressively against estate taxes, arguing that they rob first-generation high-net-worth African-Americans from passing on much of their wealth to their families. And after paying nearly $200,000 for a Ferrari Spider, Johnson dealt with more than five months of red tape to get the U.S. government to approve the shipment of the vehicle into the country from Europe.[4]

All in all, things were looking great. More than a year before his Charlotte Bobcats would tip off for the first time, Johnson was chosen by *Sports Illustrated* magazine as the "Most Influential Minority in Sports." Even Johnson's once-contentious relationship with his sister had mellowed, according to a family friend, and they could now stand to be in the same room with each other.

With their respective divorces final, Johnson and Lee were often together in public. People within BET and the entire industry were guessing how long the relationship might last, and whether Lee would ascend to the top job at BET at the expiration of Johnson's contract in 2006. In the meantime, from late-night dinners at Georgetown's ritzy Café Milano to star-studded music industry events in New York, Lee and Johnson showed up as a couple. In 2003, at the lavish party that music mogul Clive Davis throws before the Grammy awards each year, they entered together in formal attire, with Johnson on crutches nursing an Achilles tendon injury. Several months later, they joined Denzel Washington in New York for the premiere of *Out of Time*, the movie star's latest release. As Washington conducted interviews on the red carpet outside, Johnson and Lee sat together in the middle of the theater waiting for the show to begin. The billionaire mogul was surrounded by his famous best friends that night, as Butch Lewis and the actor Leon Robinson were also present. Life was good.

On the morning that Johnson was honored by the city of Los Angeles, the BET founder stood erect in the council chamber, saint-like in his all-white suit. With Lee at his side, he listened proudly as the "BET Day" proclamation was read aloud. Afterward, various city council members addressed the chamber, offering praise to Johnson. "I want to congratulate you on being a trailblazer," said one councilman. "For opening the door to all of us who seek diversity." Another councilman spoke: "Bob Johnson has made a tremendous contribution to the education of all people," he proclaimed.

Later that night, the red carpet outside the city's Kodak Theater, the new home of the prestigious Academy Awards, was baptized in black. Along Hollywood Boulevard, young people danced and screamed as stars arrived for the Second Annual BET Awards. Making their way through the crowds were new idols such as the rapper Ja Rule and the singer and songwriter Alicia Keys. There were the BET regulars like Mary J. Blige and Snoop Dogg. And there were aging superstars, including the 1970s group Earth, Wind, and Fire. Even boxing legend Muhammad Ali ambled into the theater, taking his seat near Johnson.

The show started, and the rap star Nelly appeared onstage. Huge plumes of fire shot up in the air and he began to sing: "It's getting hot in here, so take off all your clothes." Suddenly, he was surrounded by beautiful, sexy black women. They were bumping and grinding, wearing shorts cut so high that much of their perfect round bottoms were uncovered, shaking freely.

ACKNOWLEDGMENTS

When I was assigned to write the *Forbes* "400 Richest People in America" cover story on Robert Johnson in 2001, I knew it was a special opportunity. The mainstream financial media has long given short shrift to black-owned businesses and their leaders. Too often, when these businesses do receive media coverage, they are handled gingerly, not taken as seriously or scrutinized as closely as their mainstream counterparts. There are exceptions to this observation, but not nearly enough of them. This book evolved from that story, so I am thankful to my editors at *Forbes* for first recognizing that Johnson deserved to be on the cover, and for then allowing me to go off and write this book.

To Bob Johnson, who chose not to participate on this project but was helpful by providing earlier interviews, I thank you. Fortunately, I was able to draw from those earlier conversations, which included two interviews in person (one was on background, not for quoting) and two telephone conversations. Unfortunately, when I later tried to discuss this book with Johnson, he refused my every attempt and repeated over and over again, "I have no interest."

However, because Johnson has become a supremely successful entrepreneur and did it by developing a product that is in millions of homes, many people want to know about him and his company. And they have every right to know. This is why I have written this book. Although it was written without Johnson's cooperation, I have made every attempt to be comprehensive and fair, and I am honored to have chronicled his story.

This is the result of two years of research and writing and more than 75 interviews. Many people have been very generous with their time and with information. I thank them. Some people chose to cooperate even after Johnson asked them not to do so. I am grateful for their courage. Others abided by his wishes and refused to talk. I respect their decision. And then there were those who, citing possible retribution, agreed to cooperate only if they could remain anonymous. I have granted their requests.

Some of the interviews used for this book took place when I was researching magazine stories. I have made note of this whenever such conversations are cited. Also, live dialogue in the book has been reconstructed based on the memories of people who were present when the conversations took place. This is not an exact science, as people tend to have selective memories. This shortcoming is a reality of journalism, a limitation of the craft. Still, every effort has been made to verify and properly attribute all dialogue.

This book would have never been completed without the assistance, encouragement, and prayers of so many. Those people are too numerous to list by name, yet I am grateful to each of them. There are some, however, who were too vital to the process to go unmentioned. Clarita Jones, in the *Forbes* information center, provided invaluable research assistance. Clio Morgan transcribed hours of interviews. My father-in-law, Taylor Hightower, lent me his weekend home on the New Jersey shore, where I found quiet isolation and wrote much of the manuscript. And my lifelong friend, Kevin Chase, allowed me to turn his condo into my office whenever I was conducting research in the Washington, D.C., area. Randy Thompson provided his expert legal counsel. David Dickerson shared his abundant Rolodex and keen insight. Josie Lee guided me through the world of show horses. Olga Carlile showed me around Freeport, Illinois. Jason Miccolo Johnson, Welton Doby, and the staff at The Cable Center in Denver helped me round up photographs. Cable industry analyst Derek Baine provided some financial research. And my mother-in-law, Sandra Hightower, has been my fervent promoter, touting this book long before a single word was ever written. Others who helped in myriad ways include my friends Kenny Walker, George Mapp, Richard Walton, Ivan Thornton, Steve Ramos, and Myke Freeman.

I am most appreciative of my fellow word merchants, who gave generously of their time and expertise—vetting this manuscript, suggesting important alterations, correcting, tweaking, and critiquing: Frank James and Vickie Walton of the *Chicago Tribune* and Johnnie Roberts of *Newsweek* are each among the best at their craft.

To my agent, Djana Pearson Morris: Thanks for finding me, and for believing from day one in my ability and in this project. To Jeanne Glasser, my editor at John Wiley & Sons: Thanks so much for taking on this first-time author.

Last but not least, I thank my family: my late father, Charles Pulley, who taught me the virtue of hard work and the enduring obligation to those you love; my mother, Jean Pulley, who told me to never be slowed down by looking back and to trust that with faith, all things are possible; my sisters, Angela Hill and Melanie Blagburn, who have protected me, taught me, and helped me polish this book; and my best friends—my wife, Stacey, and daughters, Zoë and Blake, who have been right there each step of the way, navigating this process with me. I'm so glad we are on this journey together.

NOTES

PROLOGUE: "BOOTYLICIOUS"

1. Author interview with Robert Johnson for article "Cable Capitalist," *Forbes*, October 8, 2001.
2. 2003 BET Awards, June 24, 2003.

1 THE OTHER SIDE OF THE TRACKS

1. Robert Johnson and Brian Dumaine, "The Market Nobody Wanted," *Fortune Small Business*, October 1, 2002.
2. Ibid.
3. Author interview with Preston Pearson, January 9, 2003.
4. Marlo Thomas, *The Right Words at the Right Time*, New York: Atria Books, 2002.
5. Ibid.
6. Author interview with Robert Johnson for *Forbes* magazine, 2001.
7. The author is also one of more than 75,000 living members of Kappa Alpha Psi.

2 ACCESS TO POWER

1. Author interview with Walter Fauntroy, September 16, 2002.
2. Author interview with Delano Lewis, 2003.
3. Robert Johnson and Brian Dumaine, "The Market Nobody Wanted," *Fortune Small Business*, October 1, 2002.
4. Ibid.
5. Mark Robichaux, *Cable Cowboy*, Hoboken, NJ: John Wiley & Sons, 2002.

6. *Billboard/Hollywood Reporter*, BET 20th anniversary special edition, 2000.
7. The Cable Center, Denver, Colorado—from the Center's oral history collection of taped interviews with industry pioneers.
8. Johnson has recounted that Silverman told him of his plan on the way to a meeting at Claude Pepper's office. However, Silverman says he and Johnson never actually visited Pepper together.
9. Vivian Goodier, civil complaint, 1992.

3   "WHITE MAN, CAN YOU SPARE HALF A MILLION?"

1. *Fortune Small Business*, October 1, 2002.
2. *Multichannel News*, BET special supplement, 2000.
3. *BET Celebrating Twenty Years of Black Star Power*, Washington, DC: BET Books, 2000, page 21.
4. Derek Dingle, *Lessons from the Top*, New York: John Wiley & Sons, 1999, page 38.
5. *Fortune Small Business*, October 1, 2002.
6. Author interview with Robert Johnson, 1999.
7. *Multichannel News*, BET special supplement, 2000.
8. Author interview with Virgil Hemphill, January 8, 2003.
9. Paulette Johnson deposition, from 1992 complaint.

4   REVEREND ELDORADO

1. Author interview with Tim Reid, August 20, 2002.
2. Author interviews with Don Anderson, 2002 and 2003.
3. Author interview with Alvin Jones, 2002.
4. Ibid.
5. Ibid.
6. Ibid.
7. From John Malone's deposition, 1992.
8. Author interview with Robin Beamon, March 24, 2003.

9. From Paulette Johnson's deposition, 1992.
10. Ibid. Note that while Paulette never publicly admitted any wrongdoing, the public court files contain her promissory note to repay the money, as well as notes from her concerning her credit card charges.

5 COUNTRY BOY CHARM, PREDATOR'S HEART

1. Author interview with Don Anderson, 2003.
2. Ibid.
3. Peter Perl, "His Way," *Washington Post*, December 14, 1997.
4. John Johnson was out on medical leave and declined to be interviewed for this book.
5. Author interview with Michael Fuchs, 2003.
6. Author interview with Tim Reid, 2003.
7. Ibid.

6 THE FAMILY

1. Author interview with Curtis Gadson, 2001.
2. Author interview with Madelyne Woods, January 28, 2003.
3. Author interview with David Grain, 2003.
4. Author interview with Curtis Symonds, 2002.

7 "BET IN THE HOUSE"

1. Author interview with Jefferi Lee, 2001.
2. Leon Wynter, "Business and Race," *Wall Street Journal*, December 24, 1991.
3. Ibid.
4. Stan Hinden, *Washington Post*, November 1, 1991.
5. Derek Dingle, *Lessons from the Top*, New York: John Wiley & Sons, 1999, page 31.

6. Author interview with Mario Gabelli, 2003.
7. *Johnson vs. Johnson*, 1992, complaint.
8. Author interview with Virgil Hemphill, 2002.
9. Paulette Johnson deposition, *Johnson vs. Johnson*, 1992.
10. Author interview with Sheila Johnson, 2002.

8   SHAKIN' IT . . . SMACKIN' IT

1. Richard Harrington, "Boycott of MCA Ended," *Washington Post*, July 12, 1991.
2. Tom McGrath, *MTV: The Making of a Revolution*, Philadelphia: Running Press, 1996.
3. Author interview with Don Anderson, 2002.
4. Author interview with Tom Joyner, 2001.
5. Peter Perl, "His Way," *Washington Post*, December 14, 1997.
6. Author interview with Jefferi Lee, 2001.
7. *60 Minutes*, CBS, April 4, 1999.
8. Brett Nelson, "The Inside Track," *Forbes*, October 18, 1999.
9. Author interview with Richard Parsons, 1995.
10. Author interview with Robert Johnson, 2001.

9   "TIRED OL' RERUNS"

1. BET 1996 annual report.
2. Author interview with Jefferi Lee, 2001.
3. Allison Samuels, "Bad Vibes at Cable's BET," *Newsweek*, October 25, 1999.
4. Vernon Clement Jones, "Not Black Like Me," *Toronto Globe and Mail*, February 19, 2001.
5. Greg Braxton, "Brouhaha over BET Continues," *Los Angeles Times*, November 28, 2001.

6. Author interview with George Curry, 2003.

7. Author interview with Curtis Gadson, 2001; as recounted to Gadson by Johnson.

8. Samuels, "Bad Vibes at Cable's BET."

9. Lee Bailey, "BET Steps Out," *Electronic Urban Report*, June 13, 2001.

10. From BET internal documents provided to author.

11. Ibid.

12. Peter Perl, "His Way," *Washington Post*, December 14, 1997.

13. Author interview with Robert Johnson, 2001.

14. Ibid.

15. Ibid.

16. Author interview with Aaron McGruder, 2002.

17. Author interview with Robert Johnson, 2001.

10   WEALTH AND POWER

1. Tariq K. Muhammad, "The Branding of BET," *Black Enterprise*, June 1997.

2. *60 Minutes*, CBS, transcript, April 4, 1999.

3. Nancy Jaffer, "For the Love of Paige," *Spur*, October 1997.

4. Alicia Mundy, "Does Bob Johnson Stand Alone?" *MediaWeek*, March 31, 1997.

5. Jaffer, "For the Love of Paige."

6. Author interview with Sheila Johnson, 2001.

7. Author interview with Paige Johnson, 2001.

8. *Crawford vs. BET*, civil complaint, August 16, 2000.

9. Phil Berger, "Lewis Promotes Himself As Well As the Fighters," *New York Times*, May 30, 1983.

10. Peter Perl, "His Way," *Washington Post*, December 14, 1997.

11. Paul Fahri, "Johnson's Dream of a Team," *Washington Post*, August 22, 1994.

12. Mundy, "Does Bob Johnson Stand Alone?"
13. Author interview with Dwight Ellis, 2002.

11   THE BLACK DISNEY

1. Author interview with Donnie Simpson, 2004.
2. *BET Celebrating Twenty Years of Black Star Power*, Washington, DC: BET Books, 2000, page 84.
3. David Whitford, "Taking BET Back from the Street," *Fortune*, November 9, 1998.
4. *Multichannel News*, "Stepping Up the Beat," 20th anniversary special, 2000.

12   COSTLY AFFAIRS

1. Author interview with Curtis Symonds.
2. This was recounted by two executives who were present at the time.
3. Author interview with Curtis Symonds.
4. Author interview with Sheila Johnson.
5. Allison Samuels, "Bad Vibes at Cable's BET," *Newsweek*, October 25, 1999.
6. This comment was recounted by sources close to Smiley.
7. Author interview with Herb Wilkins.
8. Over the years, the author of this book wrote several articles for *Emerge* and *Savoy*.
9. Author interview with Robert Johnson, 2001.
10. Ibid.
11. Ibid.

13   "SELLOUT!"

1. The meeting and conversations between Johnson and Redstone were recounted by Johnson during a 2001 interview

with author and during a November 2000 BET conference call with journalists and analysts.

2. Author interview with Debra Lee, 2001.
3. BET corporate communications; BET conference call transcript, November 3, 2000.
4. Author interview with Mel Karmazin for *Forbes*, 2001.
5. Viacom press release, November 3, 2000.
6. Yemi Toure, "BET: End of an Era," Hype Information Service, November 2000.
7. Teresa Wiltz, "But Has the Network Sold a Bit of Its Soul?," *Washington Post*, November 4, 2000.
8. Kevin Merida, "The Company He Keeps," *Washington Post*, December 17, 2000.
9. Author interview with Mel Karmazin for *Forbes*, 2001.
10. Ibid.
11. *Current Biography Yearbook* 2002, New York: H.W. Wilson Co., 2002.
12. Diane Toroian, "Protest Builds over Firing of BET Host Tavis Smiley," *St. Louis Post-Dispatch*, April 14, 2001.
13. Author interview with Tom Joyner, 2001.
14. Author interview with Mel Karmazin for *Forbes*, 2001.
15. Author interview with Tom Joyner, 2001.

14   HE GOT GAME

1. Ann Gerhart, "Out of the Shadows," *Washington Post*, May 26, 2002.
2. Author interview with Sheila Johnson, 2002.
3. Author interview with Robert Johnson, 2001.
4. Keith Alexander, "Johnson Lobbies for Merger of Airlines; BET Founder Would Run New Carrier," *Washington Post*, May 4, 2001.
5. Author interview with Robert Johnson, 2001.
6. *Black Enterprise*, "Making the Top 100," June 2003.

7. Author interview with Robert Johnson, 2001.

8. Michael Hiestand, "Winning NBA Bid Just Start," *USA Today*, December 19, 2002.

9. John Delong, "Shinn Rejects Offer for Hornets," *Winston-Salem Journal*, March 6, 2002.

10. Robert Johnson, speaking at the World Congress of Sports, New York, March 2003.

11. John Lombardo, "New Owner Must Rebuild Charlotte Market," *Sports Business Journal*, December 23–29, 2002.

12. Hiestand, "Winning NBA Bid Just Start."

13. Alan Hughes, "Slam Dunk!" *Black Enterprise*, March 2003.

14. Ibid.

15. NBA transcript of press conference, December 18, 2002.

16. Robert Johnson, speaking at the World Congress of Sports, New York, March 2003.

17. Joseph Patel, "Minority Report," *Vibe*, November 2003.

EPILOGUE: ONE NATION UNDER A GROOVE

1. Author interview with Michael Eric Dyson, 2003.

2. Jacqueline Trescott, "BET Founder Gives $3 Million to Underground Railroad Museum," *Washington Post*, February 7, 2003.

3. Author interview with Alfred Liggins, 2003.

4. Alec Klein, "Life in the Stalled Lane," *Washington Post*, January 6, 2002.

BIBLIOGRAPHY

Alexander, Keith. "Johnson Lobbies for Merger of Airlines; BET Founder Would Run New Carrier." *Washington Post* (May 4, 2001).

Bailey, Lee. "BET Steps Out." *Electronic Urban Report* (June 13, 2001).

Berger, Phil. "Lewis Promotes Himself as Well as the Fighters." *New York Times* (May 30, 1983).

BET Celebrating Twenty Years of Black Star Power (Washington, DC: BET Books, 2000).

"BET Hopes to Recover Faulty Outlay." *Daily Variety* (October 23, 1992).

"BET 20th Anniversary Salute." *Billboard* (2000).

Braxton, Greg. "Brouhaha over BET Continues." *Los Angeles Times* (November 28, 2001).

Brownlee, Lisa. "Johnson Makes $1 BET on Taking Radio Public." *New York Post* (October 27, 1999).

Current Biography Yearbook 2002, (New York: H.W. Wilson Co., 2002).

Dingle, Derek. *Lessons from the Top* (New York: John Wiley & Sons, 1999).

Fahri, Paul. "Former BET Executive Admits Fraud." *Washington Post* (January 27, 1994).

"Gabelli Filing Says BET Holdings Offer for Shares Too Low." Dow Jones News Service (October 6, 1997).

Gerhart, Ann. "Out of the Shadows." *Washington Post* (May 26, 2002).

Harrington, Richard. "Boycott of MCA Ended." *Washington Post* (July 12, 1991).

Hiestand, Michael. "Winning NBA Bid Just Start." *USA Today* (December 19, 2002).

Hughes, Alan. "Slam Dunk!" *Black Enterprise* (March 2003).

Jaffer, Nancy. "For the Love of Paige." *Spur* (October 1997).

Jones, Vernon Clement. "Not Black like Me." *Globe and Mail* (February 19, 2001).

Knight, Jerry. "For Lewis and Shareholders, BET's Buyout Offer Is Too Low." *Washington Post* (February 2, 1998).

Lee, Josephine. "Horseplay." *Forbes* (October 8, 2001).

Lombardo, John. "New Owner Must Rebuild Charlotte Market." *Sports Business Journal* (December 23–29, 2002).

Marriott, Anne. "BET Shareholder Protests Privatization Bid." *Washington Times* (October 7, 1997).

McConville, Jim. "BET Axes Plans for New Black Family Channel." *Electronic Media* (February 21, 2000).

McGrath, Tom. *MTV: The Making of a Revolution* (Philadelphia: Running Press, 1996).

McGruder, Aaron. *The Boondocks* (Kansas City, Mo.: Andrews McMeel Publishing, 2000).

Merida, Kevin. "The Company He Keeps." *Washington Post* (December 17, 2000.)

Muhammad, Tariq K. "The Branding of BET." *Black Enterprise* (June 1997).

Perl, Peter. "His Way," *Washington Post* (December 14, 1997).

Pulley, Brett. "The Cable Capitalist." *Forbes* (October 8, 2001).

Pulley, Brett. "Oprah Who?" *Forbes* (November 27, 2000).

Redstone, Sumner, and Peter Knobler. *A Passion to Win* (New York: Simon & Schuster, 2001).

Robichaux, Mark. *Cable Cowboy* (Hoboken: John Wiley & Sons, 2002).

Samuels, Allison. "Bad Vibes at Cable's BET." *Newsweek* (October 25, 1999).

Thomas, Marlo. *The Right Words at the Right Time* (New York: Atria Books, 2002).

Toroian, Diane. "Protest Builds over Firing of BET Host Tavis Smiley." *St. Louis Post-Dispatch* (April 14, 2001).

Walker, Blair. *Why Should White Guys Have All the Fun?* (New York: John Wiley & Sons, 1995).

Whitford, David. "Taking BET Back from the Street." *Fortune* (November 9, 1998).

Williams, Christopher. "A Canny BET: Viacom's Wager on Black Entertainment Should Pay Off." *Barron's* (May 7, 2001).

Zabcik, Bran. "Who's Suing Whom." *Manhattan Lawyer* (April 25, 1989).

Zagorin, Adam. "BET's Too Hot a Property." *Time* (October 20, 1997).

INDEX